England's Historic Churches by Train

Engines in the National Railway Museum, York

So still they stand inside their tomb
it seems impossible that they
should once have torn the air apart
with thunderous wheels and whistle-screams,
and we forget the awesome power
they generated in their prime.

Paint bright as morning, spick and span,
polished like antique furniture,
their names as pure as trumpet notes:
Atlantic Coast Express, Mallard,
Green Arrow, Gladstone, Evening Star.
With them an era's dead and gone.

But let imagination ride,
and once again the night is split
with furnace flame and windows lit
and smoke like mist across the fields
and in and out of stooks and ricks
slip *Red Dragon* and *Silver Fox.*

In the last days of our lost ease,
through tall forests of mill chimneys,
Queen of Scots and *Northumbrian*
were on the inter-city run
and England seemed a stable place
when *Master Cutler* ran his race.

I found this poem in an anthology of railway poetry entitled *Marigolds grow wild on platforms* compiled by Peggy Poole and first published by Cassell Publishers in 1996.

The poem was written by John Ward. I have included it here because to me it encapsulates an era when for nearly one hundred and fifty years steam locomotives and those who drove and fired them, provided the bedrock of the railway system. The names in italics are either those of named trains which ran across Britain or famous locomotives which in their heyday would have been well known to the travelling public.

Author

England's Historic Churches by Train

A Companion Volume to
England's Cathedrals by Train

Murray Naylor

First published in Great Britain in 2016 by
Remember When
an imprint of
Pen & Sword Books Ltd
47 Church Street
Barnsley
South Yorkshire
S70 2AS

ISBN 978 1 47387 142 7

Typeset in Ehrhardt by
Mac Style, Bridlington, East Yorkshire
Printed and bound by Replika Press Pvt. Ltd.

Pen & Sword Books Ltd incorporates the imprints of Pen & Sword Archaeology,
Atlas, Aviation, Battleground, Discovery, Family History, History, Maritime,
Military, Naval, Politics, Railways, Select, Social History, Transport, True Crime, and
Claymore Press, Frontline Books, Leo Cooper, Praetorian Press, Remember When,
Seaforth Publishing and Wharncliffe.

For a complete list of Pen & Sword titles please contact
PEN & SWORD BOOKS LIMITED
47 Church Street, Barnsley, South Yorkshire, S70 2AS, England
E-mail: enquiries@pen-and-sword.co.uk
Website: www.pen-and-sword.co.uk

Contents

Acknowledgements

I am indebted to a number of people for the assistance I have received in writing this book. Encouragement has come from several quarters, not least the reassurance I gained from the success of *England's Cathedrals by Train* which emboldened me to consider a follow-up title covering a different but equally important group of Anglican churches.

I am particularly grateful to Doctor Ronald Clayton, recently retired from York University and a fellow guide at York Minster for reading the manuscript and giving wise advice as to content and construction. The vicars of two of the churches featured and nearest to where I live – Beverley Minster and Selby Abbey – gave me their personal time and made useful comments on the script for which I am grateful, as did a number of others whom I consulted. I have also received help with photographs and maps and would wish to thank those who have supplied a number; as an amateur photographer I find composing images of trains and the often dark interiors of churches a challenge. My thanks too to Mrs Carol Trow for her assiduous work in editing the manuscript.

Finally I am grateful to Bishop James Newcome for agreeing to write a foreword. I approached him just before widespread flooding inundated many of the communities in his Carlisle diocese in early December 2015 and I am sure, as he attended to their wellbeing, the last thing he would have wished was a commitment to write something for me. His kind words are testimony to the trouble he so clearly took.

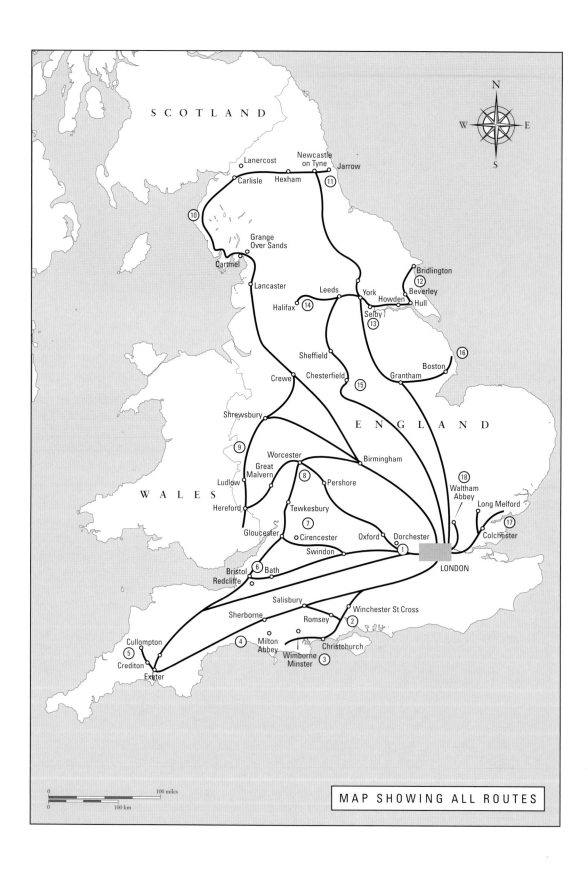

MAP SHOWING ALL ROUTES

Foreword

by the Rt Revd James Newcome, The Bishop of Carlisle

Murray Naylor's companion book to *England's Cathedrals by Train* is excellent. His selection of thirty-two churches out of a possible sixteen thousand is both thoughtful and imaginative. By selecting churches for their interest and merit he does not seek to be comprehensive, rather to link entertaining train journeys with spectacular destinations. This book is no dull architectural survey but rather a lively perambulation with the author around some of the most interesting corners of England.

Of particular interest to me is Mr Naylor's description of Cartmel and Lanercost Priories in Chapter Ten. Both of these fine churches are in the diocese of Carlisle and have had many books written about them, but rarely with any mention of 'La'al Ratty'. That Cumbrian dialect phrase describes the 'little railway' which Mr Naylor fondly describes running up Eskdale and which he links with these two spectacular buildings.

Mr Naylor's new book is a joy to read. It will delight those who delved into his earlier work and encourage all who read it to take a leisurely train to savour visits to these lovely churches. I warmly recommend this book to all readers who love churches and railways.

James Newcome

List of Illustrations

The Author has taken all possible steps to check the architectural and chronological details given in the book. He accepts responsibility for any inaccuracies that remain.

Unless otherwise stated, all illustrations have been provided by the author.

Summary of Railway Notes

1. Building on Brunel to deliver a modern railway.
2. New approaches to providing services and developing rail freight.
3. Line closures by Beeching and their destiny fifty years later.
4. The carriage of passengers.
5. A train driver's responsibilities. Dawlish 2014.
6. Tunnelling and the Severn Tunnel.
7. What causes service disruption.
8. Bridges and Viaducts. The Severn Valley Railway.
9. Railway signalling and the Quintinshill disaster.
10. Carriage of hazardous materials. The Ravenglass & Eskdale narrow gauge railway.
11. The birth of railways. The creation of the Tyne & Wear Metro.
12. Local railways in East Yorkshire.
13. The Selby avoiding line. Some observations on overseas rail travel.
14. The Pacer and urban networks.
15. The further electrification of the railways. George Stephenson's burial place.
16. Railway towns – Crewe.
17. The future for railways across the world.
18. Modernising London's railway infrastructure.

Author's Note

My book, *England's Cathedrals by Train: Discover How the Normans and the Victorians Helped to Shape Our Lives* was published in 2013. It took readers on a series of journeys around England to visit thirty-three of our great Anglican cathedrals. The journeys were made exclusively by train and, in addition to providing a short history and description of each cathedral visited, the book also added historical and contemporary information about Britain's railway system. Underlying what I wrote was a wish to draw the attention of the reader to the achievements of two remarkable periods in our Nation's history; the Norman era after the Conquest and the Victorian epoch in the nineteenth century.

England's Great Historic Churches by Train is a companion book. It follows the same form as *England's Cathedrals by Train*, albeit focusing on a different group of churches. There are approximately 16,000 churches in the Church of England and it would be unrealistic to expect to include more than a very small number in a book of this description, which I wanted to reflect the previous book in purpose and style. I therefore selected thirty-two churches which caught my attention: some are great abbeys or priories which can rival our cathedrals in their size and magnificence; some are churches still styled a minster, while others are parish churches of no particular distinction but which provided a special interest for me. In choosing my churches, I set myself certain criteria; these included identifying a wide geographical spread of places across England, thereby allowing me to make journeys similar to those in *England's Cathedrals by Train*, while giving access by railway to within fifteen miles of each place visited. Only Milton Abbey lies beyond that limit.

My descriptions are aimed at uncovering aspects of each church which may not be immediately obvious to a visitor, particularly anyone with little time at their disposal. I have also given some information on a building's history and the turbulent times they may have lived through over the centuries. I have provided only outline architectural information, preferring that a reader be advised by an official guide book, of which the larger churches usually have excellent copies, or a more academic work. In summary, the book is one into which I visualise a reader delving, as and when they wish or when they are planning a visit.

Presentation of information appropriate to railways follows a similar pattern to that in *England's Cathedrals by Train*. The subjects I have chosen cover historical development and existing practice, while attempting in places to give a personal view as to where the future may lead the railway industry. I believe that future could be exciting and entirely beneficial if we have the determination to grasp the opportunities which could arise. Finally, I hope readers will find my railway comments helpful to give a more informed understanding of the complexities of managing a modern railway network, in an age when the customer rightly expects much of the provider, but has little understanding of the operational challenges which the latter must invariably face from time to time.

Murray Naylor,
North Yorkshire
November 2015

Freight train on the Mid Hants Railway. (Steve Morley)

Preface

The Dissolution

As you travel around England visiting some or maybe all the churches recorded in this book, keep in mind one event in the first half of the sixteenth century which affected almost all of them. In 1509 Henry VIII succeeded to the English throne. Following some uneventful early years, his reign gradually degenerated into a series of programmes aimed ultimately at reducing the status, power and wealth of the Roman Catholic Church in England. A failure by the King's first wife, Catherine of Aragon, to give him a male heir and the subsequent refusal by the Vatican to grant a divorce, prompted Henry to break England away from the Papacy. In 1534 the Act of Supremacy declaring that England was in future to be an empire, governed by 'one Head and King', was passed with the support of an anti-clerical parliament. From that time Westminster began to make laws relevant to religious practice and doctrine, matters previously authorised by the Church alone. There then followed probably the most drastic revolution in English history when Henry ordered the monasteries to be dissolved, their wealth to be confiscated and their monks to be dispersed. This action, master minded on the King's behalf by Thomas Cromwell, his Chief Minister, resulted in the virtual destruction of the old religious order and its eventual replacement, after further years of dissent and disruption, by the Church of England. The Dissolution provides the backcloth for much in this book.

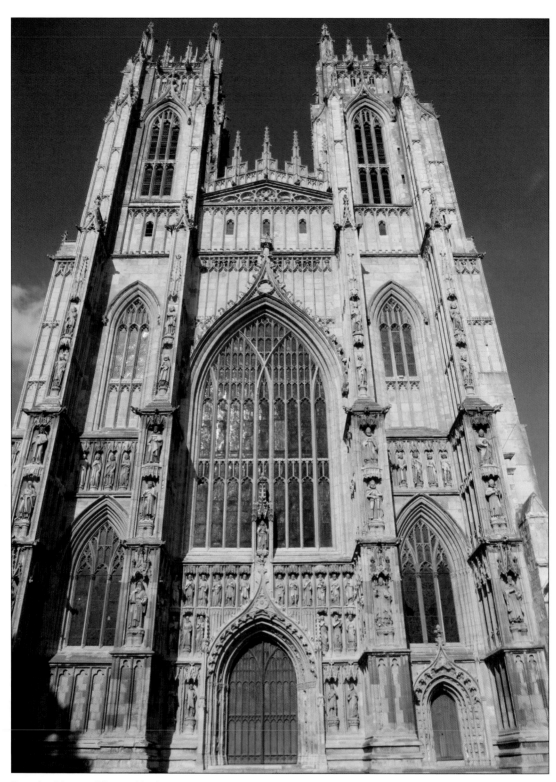

Beverley Minster. (Mervyn King)

The Journey

All journeys in this book start from the London rail terminal appropriate to the route to be taken to reach the English county in which churches are located; however not every church selected for inclusion can be reached directly by rail from London and a change of trains or use of a motor vehicle may be required. Before commencing a journey, the traveller should take a little time to get to know and admire the terminal from which his or her train departs. Strenuous efforts have been made in recent years to improve the ambience and utility of several London main line stations, those at King's Cross and Paddington now providing a much better 'traveller experience' than in the past. Others, like Euston, remain to be enhanced, something which should happen before the High Speed Two route is completed. The parallel between the nation's principal stations, both in London and in the provinces – their grandeur as constructions of steel and glass meriting a description of 'railway cathedrals' – suggests comparison with some of the churches included in this book, built in different materials in different eras but equally cathedral-like in their magnificence.

One of Britain's great modern stations, Manchester Piccadilly.

As in *England's Cathedrals by Train*, journeys start to the west of the capital, first visiting the abbey at Dorchester on Thames, thereafter radiating clockwise to finish at Waltham Abbey on the fringes of North East London. I have included some of the great medieval churches, which, had historical events happened differently, might today be cathedrals and the seat of a diocesan bishop; numbered amongst these are the wonderful buildings at Beverley in East Yorkshire and at Tewkesbury in Gloucestershire. Other churches of great historical distinction and pronounced beauty are St Mary, Redcliffe in Bristol and Great Malvern Priory in Worcestershire while Cartmel and Lanercost, both priories in Cumbria, deserve a mention for what they tell us about the northern extremities of Britain in the turbulent years when the kings of England and Scotland fought for supremacy over the Border lands. St Paul's Church at Jarrow, close to the mouth of the river Tyne, is included because of its historical association with St Bede, while Chesterfield's Crooked Spire church and the Stump at Boston in Lincolnshire are numbered amongst buildings with a particularly interesting history, the latter being the starting point for some of the first pilgrims to sail for the New World in the seventeenth century. The abbey churches at Selby, Bath and Sherborne all merit inclusion in my list for their elegance and culture as does St Cross in Winchester, one of the oldest alms houses in the country; all are important for their contribution to history and the roles they have performed in most cases for nearly a thousand years or indeed longer, in helping to sustain the Christian faith in these islands.

A cross country service from the Midlands to Eastern England.

South East

Dorchester on Thames Abbey.

The East window, Dorchester Abbey.

Chapter 1

Oxfordshire

■ Building on Brunel to deliver a modern railway ■ **Dorchester on Thames Abbey** ■

Getting There

Dorchester lies in the Thames valley and is easily reached by a train from London Paddington to Didcot Parkway. A fast service takes approximately forty minutes and trains are numerous. While there are intermediate stations between Didcot and Oxford, with some trains stopping at Culham and Radley, both closer to Dorchester than Didcot, they are less frequent and can take up to one and a half hours from London. Dorchester Abbey is about five miles from Didcot Station and a taxi from the latter is recommended.

Railway Notes

Isambard Kingdom Brunel was responsible for building much of the former Great Western Railway which was eventually to extend from Paddington Station in West London westwards to serve the West of England, South Wales, the Cotswolds and parts of the West Midlands. Originally built to a broad gauge of 7ft ¼ in between the rails, Brunel's routes were meticulously engineered with much of the survey work being carried out by Brunel himself. The main line west from London follows the Thames valley almost to Swindon and has been described as 'billiard table' flat, allowing the achievement from the earliest days of high speeds with minimum demand being placed upon the steam locomotives built to provide the haulage. Brunel's achievements as a civil engineer and a builder of ships, railways and stations are comprehensively recorded in several chapters of *England's Cathedrals by Train*. It bears repeating that, although he lived for only fifty-three years, in his lifetime Brunel probably achieved more than either his contemporaries or his counterparts today and that he did it with little or none of the technical support now taken for granted. He was one of Britain's greatest engineers, if not the greatest.

By 2033 Brunel's railway will be approaching its two hundredth anniversary. While engineering and scientific invention have allowed his original lines to be modernised and improved, the basic design of the railway remains much as he built it. Successive developments in motive power, beginning with steam engines, later to be replaced by diesel locomotives, themselves to be displaced in time by electric power, have all led to travel by train becoming faster, more comfortable and cleaner while traffic pinch points along Brunel's railway have been gradually eliminated, resulting in more efficient train operations and improved reliability. Reading station, an important junction thirty-six miles west of London, is the latest example of where the upgraded infrastructure will permit the elimination of several potential conflicts, which had previously resulted in trains from one direction impeding others coming from another. An example of this work – a new 2,000 metre long viaduct immediately west of Reading Station costing £100 million – has been installed to remove a major bottleneck thereby easing the flow and reliability of rail traffic.

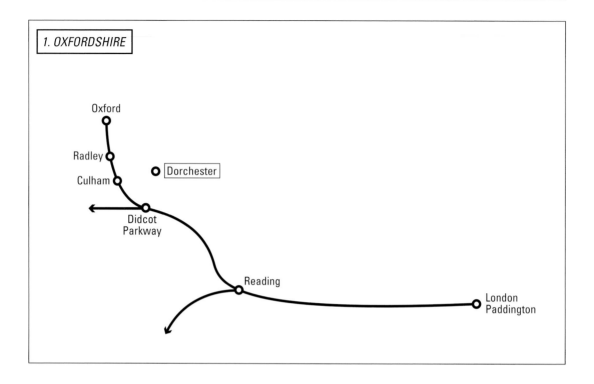

1. OXFORDSHIRE

Oxford
Radley
Culham
Dorchester
Didcot Parkway
Reading
London Paddington

Work on building the new flyover at Reading with a First Great Western HST approaching from Bristol. (Colin J. Marsden)

A Great Western locomotive built in the early twentieth century, now preserved on the Severn Valley Railway.

As the example above demonstrates, railways and the civil engineering structures to carry them are expensive to build and maintain and the public rightly expects value for the money invested in improvements. In recent years the travelling public has shown a growing inclination to use railways in preference to undertaking journeys by road or air. Numbers of passengers have grown exponentially but this does not always reflect a preference for rail travel over other modes, rather an acceptance that alternative systems could be less reliable or convenient. However, demand for services is increasing relentlessly, with the rail network already overloaded and in many places lacking modernisation while expected to deliver higher standards of comfort, punctuality and information, struggling to keep pace. Government-initiated changes to the way rail services should be delivered in future were approved in the late 1990s, as a result of which, the industry was reorganised. Service provision was placed in the hands of private companies, many with only limited previous experience in public transport, while responsibility for railway infrastructure was vested in Network Rail, a quasi-national service. It has recently been taken into full government ownership.

The verdict on these changes credits the operating companies with achieving considerable success in providing modern trains, enhanced information, more attractive stations and a generally better rapport with the public. There is also growing evidence of operational innovation in the planning of new routes reflecting a willingness to give the public new travel opportunities. However, the success of these efforts will always depend upon an equally effective service from Network Rail, charged with managing the infrastructure and ensuring its efficient operation.

Meanwhile the challenges for the railway industry continue unabated. One industry magazine calculated that over four quarters in 2014/15 passenger growth was 4.4 per cent. Placing this increase in perspective it said 'in total 1,614 million journeys were made representing an additional 69 million trips, an average of 190,000 extra users.' The demands placed on the operators are approaching a point which may be beyond the physical capacity of our existing railways without further and considerable investment.

A steam locomotive built in 1935 at the Vulcan Foundry in Lancashire for the Chinese Railways. It weighed 195 tonnes and carried 12.2 tonnes of coal and 29,000 litres of water.

Dorchester on Thames Abbey

Nearly 1400 years old it was once the site of a Saxon cathedral, then an Augustinian abbey and is today a village church.

Look for the lead font, the glass at the east end and the shrine area with its alabaster figures from the thirteenth century.

Dorchester, one of a number of villages clustered along the banks of the river Thames south of Oxford, may once have been the capital of Wessex. The first Church was founded by St Birinus in Saxon times and was accorded cathedral status in 635 for a short period before the responsibilities of the bishop were transferred to Winchester.

Thereafter, the church had a series of different functions, including from 870 when it became the centre for a new diocese responsible for an area from the Thames to the Humber, until in 1140 it was eventually re-founded as an Augustinian Abbey by the Bishop of Lincoln. It remained an abbey until 1536 when, on the orders of Henry VIII, the abbey was dissolved and the monastic house closed. It has been the local parish church ever since and its history covers 1,400 years.

I visited Dorchester on a lovely spring day in April 2015. The abbey church stands just above a flood plain between the rivers Thame and Thames a few hundred yards above their confluence, in a tranquil church yard which seems to reflect the historical importance of the site as an early

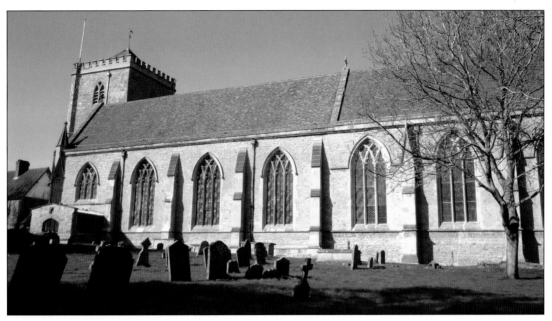

Dorchester on Thames Abbey.

Effigy of a medieval knight drawing his sword,

The Jesse window.

The Font.

cradle of English Christianity. Indeed, its long history reflecting many aspects of how the early church established itself in Britain, fully entitles it to head this first chapter

My first impression on entering the church was of a rather austere building with little embellishment and a minimum of stained glass, an impression added to by the fact that considerable work was in progress to renovate the interior, including rewiring, redecoration and the installing of new pews and stalls. Once finished, this work will no doubt allow the abbey to regain the atmosphere which rightly accords it a position as a site of great historical importance and as a place of special local worship.

The major part of the church was constructed in the twelfth century by Bishop Alexander of Lincoln; his was a simple design, cruciform in shape, without side aisles. In 1225 some relics purporting to be those of St Birinus were transferred from Winchester and the abbey became a place of pilgrimage, generating considerable income which allowed various additions to be made, including north and south choir aisles, the west tower and a shrine for the saint's relics. In 1340 the sanctuary was added with its Jesse window.

Jesse windows feature in many churches in England and on the Continent and reference to them will be made in several chapters of this book. A window usually takes the form of a vine depicting Christ's lineage growing out of Jesse, usually seen recumbent at the base, thereafter going up through his son King David, shown holding a harp, and further up –usually through Solomon and Josiah – to Mary the mother of Jesus, with Christ at the top. If there are side windows the lancets may be painted with figures representing the prophets and Kings of Judah. Christ's family tree is described in both St Matthew's and St Luke's gospels where the forty three generations said to have separated Jesse and Christ are recorded. Portrayals of the tree appear in many forms, painted in stained glass, carved in stone or printed on parchment in bibles or other religious manuscripts.

Apart from the destruction of St Birinus's shrine the church suffered relatively little damage from the ravages of the Reformation, mainly because a local knight, Sir Richard Beauforest of Dorchester, paid Henry VIII the value of the lead on the roof thereby saving the church for the local people. A hundred years later, Cromwell's troops destroyed some images and evidence of the damage can still be seen. In 1602 the tower was rebuilt and in the eighteenth and nineteenth centuries major repairs were carried out, and again in the 1960s and 1970s when a national appeal and an appeal to the American Friends of Dorchester Abbey allowed major refurbishment to be undertaken. As already noted, the programme of restoration still goes on as the church's own literature makes clear, 'to put the building into good repair, make it warm and welcoming and suited to a wide variety of uses, both religious and secular.'

Traditionally, the baptismal font has always been placed near the principal entrance to a church in order to welcome new adherents to the faith and that at Dorchester is close to the south door. It is one of the few lead fonts remaining in England and dates from around 1170. The casting around the sides shows eleven figures, thought to be the apostles, one of whom has been identified as St Peter, who can be seen carrying his key. The stone base is Victorian. The design of the font allows the 'holy' water to drain directly into the ground beneath it thus ensuring that it cannot be used for 'improper' purposes, something which was apt to happen in times past!

The south aisle adjacent to the chancel contains the Shrine Area. Speculation has it that this might have been the site of St Birinus's shrine prior to its destruction in 1536, when pilgrimage was outlawed by Henry VIII. The modern shrine was erected in the last century to commemorate Gerald Allen, the first suffragan Bishop of Dorchester when that appointment was reintroduced in 1939. The shrine area also includes a number of medieval effigies dating from the thirteenth century, which are said to be amongst the finest monuments of that period in the country. The best preserved is that of William de Valence, a nephew of Henry III, who died fighting alongside his cousin Edward I in Wales; he lies recumbent on one side, his legs crossed and with a lion at his feet, apparently twisting in the act of trying to draw his sword. There are three other similar monuments including a justice of the peace, a knight and a Saxon bishop although none are as well preserved as the effigy of de Valence. The south aisle also contains a fourteenth century wall painting of St Christopher; much faded, it would possibly have been painted over several times and was not finally revealed until 2006.

There are a number of chapels adjacent to the main part of the nave, including one dedicated to St Birinus, whose image appears in some of the windows in the church. The east window dates from 1340 and portrays scenes from the life of Christ. Unfortunately a central buttress had to be inserted after its construction to reinforce the fabric reducing the amount of glass, some of which had subsequently to be replaced by the Victorians; notwithstanding, the window is a delight to look at with sculpted scenes on some areas of the tracery.

Other windows worthy of study are the south window containing heraldic shields of the thirteenth century and the Jesse window on the north side of the chancel. Some images, including that of the Virgin and her Child and Christ in Majesty were damaged by Cromwell's soldiers in the seventeenth century. Restoration has since been carried out.

Dorchester's history, the simplicity of its interior, the fine if altered windows at the east end and the church's location in a peaceful village setting, seemingly remote from the hurly-burly of life in the modern world, makes the abbey church a satisfying and most enjoyable place to visit. The *Collins Guide to English Parish Churches*, edited by John Betjeman and published in 1958, speaks of the abbey and '….its remaining traces of distinction proper to one of the oldest of English cities. The Abbey Church, approached through a Butterfield lychgate is splendid in its proportions and detail.' The building's significance as a reflection of how the fortunes of the early church were sustained and later forfeited over a number of centuries is easy to appreciate.

Chapter 2

Hampshire

■ New approaches to providing services and developing rail freight
■ **St Cross Church, Winchester** ■ **Romsey Abbey** ■

Getting There

The city of Winchester is on the main line from London Waterloo to Southampton. The journey time is about fifty-five minutes. St Cross Church is a short distance south of the city by taxi or bus.

However Romsey, ten miles to the west of Winchester and also served by a railway, has no direct trains from London. It can be reached either via a change at Salisbury (one hour and twenty minutes from London) or via Eastleigh (one hour and ten minutes from London). On arrival at either of these stations change into a local service for the short journey to Romsey Station from where it is feasible to walk to the abbey. An alternative would be to take a taxi or bus from Eastleigh or Salisbury.

Railway Notes

The twenty years since the passing of the act of parliament which paved the way for the partial privatisation of Britain's railways in the 1990s has seen enormous change, both in terms of increasing efficiency in the handling of greater numbers of trains and passengers and in the way in which the rail network has again come to be viewed as a national asset, a far cry from the days of the Beeching era thirty years before when rail was assumed by many as being firmly in decline. As highlighted in the previous chapter more people than ever now use our railways and they expect a transport system both punctual and inexpensive; sadly such aspirations will never be fully delivered and criticism can be unforgiving. Given the difficult balance to be achieved between costs and revenue in an industry which demands high standards of safety and massive investment – again discussed in the previous chapter – it is perhaps unsurprising that railways are often viewed in a less than favourable light by the travelling public

In managing our existing railways to achieve maximum benefit, Network Rail, the national body charged with organising the infrastructure and signalling systems, tends to give operational priority to passengers over freight. Except in times of war this has applied since the days of steam but attitudes may soon change. Freight transportation is becoming ever more efficient; longer trains carrying heavier loads at sustained high speeds and the planned electrification of further key routes mean that freight trains can often match their passenger counterparts in terms of operational performance. Such developments inevitably place increased pressure on the railway infrastructure and make controlling the network an ever more demanding responsibility.

Nowhere is this pressure more visible than in Southern Hampshire. For example, the two track railway serving Southampton Docks, the military port at Marchwood and the oil refinery at

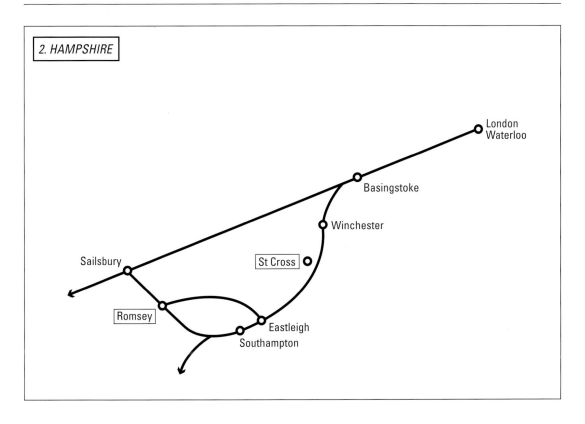

2. HAMPSHIRE

London
Waterloo

Basingstoke

Winchester

Sailsbury

St Cross

Romsey

Eastleigh
Southampton

A Freightliner passing Oxford en route from Leeds to Southampton. (Colin J Marsden)

A South West train in the New Forest.

Mid Hants Railway. (Steve Morley)

Fawley is used for the rail transport of bulk commodities as well as passenger traffic. Containers, oil tankers – some weighing up to 100 tons fully loaded – and cars destined for import and export are all moved to or from the docks by this single artery and freight journeys must be dovetailed to fit the schedules of express services and commuter trains. It is little wonder that when failures occur they can cause disruption out of proportion.

The case for the building of a new high speed line up the spine of Britain from London to the north has now been launched by the Government and a debate as to the necessity for a new line and the consequences of its construction are now being vigorously discussed, particularly in those parts of the country which will be directly affected. If ever built the line will be used primarily for high speed passenger traffic but will as a consequence free up classic routes for other traffic including freight. Meanwhile the construction of a further high speed line across the Pennines between Manchester and Leeds has also been proposed. These developments could be important if Britain is to continue to be able to move people and commercial traffic freely around the country. Equally relevant is the beneficial effect a network of fast intercity routes could have in connecting the cities of Northern England to one another to form an economic hub to rival London and the South East, and indeed Scotland. Handled correctly these challenges could redress years of decline and help to adjust the balance between the south and the north of the British Isles. Surely it behoves a country whose Victorian ancestors constructed the early railways, to build upon their success and to consider a 'new' transport revolution, when design and technology may provide the opportunity to do so?

St Cross Church, Winchester

The church and hospital stand two miles south of Winchester.

Look for the hospital buildings which cluster around the church, the massive Norman pillars in the nave, the reredos at the east end and the floor tiles in the vicinity of the chancel. Enjoy the peaceful ambience of the foundation's surrounding gardens and lawns.

Southampton Water, a few miles to the south of Winchester, is fed by two rivers. The river Itchen flows across Hampshire from the east and passes Winchester and then St Cross where the church stands adjacent to the water meadows south of the city. Fifteen miles to the west runs the river Test which rises in the north of the county, passing Romsey on its way to the sea. Romsey Abbey is the other church to feature in this chapter.

The Hospital of St Cross is probably England's oldest charitable institution. History has it that the original hospital was founded by Henry of Blois, a grandson of William the Conqueror and half-brother of Stephen, King of England between 1132 and 1136. When he was Bishop of Winchester, Henry decided to establish a secular foundation which originally consisted of thirteen brothers. Later, other deserving poor people were fed every day at the gates of the church, following completion of much of the building about 1330. The original purpose of the foundation is given in the St Cross visitor guide as being to provide accommodation for 'Thirteen poor men feeble and so reduced in strength that they can scarcely, or not at all support themselves without other aid.' Today, there are twenty-five brothers living in the alms house, around the quadrangle,

St Cross Church, Winchester.

World War One battlefield cross.

receiving broadly similar privileges to their forbears; they wear black or red robes and trencher hats - square, floppy caps - when attending church services or formal events and are led by a Master.

The original construction of St Cross began with the quire about 1160 with final completion of the nave vault in 1408. The institution has always benefitted from the patronage of wealthy backers. John de Campden was Master of the foundation in the late fourteenth century and made several alterations to the church. Another benefactor, Cardinal Beaufort, another Bishop of Winchester in the following century, extended the hospital with an alms house, establishing a second foundation in 1445 – the Order of Noble Poverty – to give support for gentry who had fallen upon hard times. The church is beautifully proportioned despite the length of time it took to construct and the various architectural periods which pertained over the period of its building.

However, several changes took place in later centuries, in particular when Richard Fox was the Bishop and commissioned new quire stalls; sadly, many of these were destroyed in the nineteenth

Victorian tiling showing the letters 'ZO'.

century. The church is notable for its massive Norman pillars, several adorned with chevrons, the height of some in the nave reaching to clerestory level. Much later, the quire was restored by William Butterfield in 1860 when the reredos behind the altar was installed.

There is a useful guide in the church to tell the visitor what to look for. The wall at the east end depicts four figures. Appropriately, because of their geographic relevance, are included St Swithun, a ninth century bishop buried close by at Winchester Cathedral and whose story is recounted in Chapter 4 of *England's Cathedrals by Train*, and St Catherine, the patron saint of wheel-wrights whose name adorns a hill above the city. They are accompanied by statues of the Virgin Mary and St John the Baptist. Meanwhile, the Lady Chapel contains a triptych dating from about 1520 which shows Joseph and Mary fleeing into exile in Egypt. On the north side opposite the Lady Chapel, the War Memorial Chapel contains a wooden battlefield cross which was used to mark the burial place of Captain Russell of the 12th Rifle Brigade when he was killed in action in Flanders on 7 October 1916.

Some of the surviving tiles in the two chapels either side of the chancel are said to be the medieval originals laid in the fourteenth century. Others have been replaced with Victorian replicas. A number in the chancel are embossed with the letters ZO. It is thought that these tiles were donated anonymously but that the donor could have been Edward, Prince of Wales, who apparently often used to call in at St Cross when travelling to Osborne House in the Isle of Wight to visit his mother, Queen Victoria, around 1860. It is claimed that he may have often signed himself with the two letters ZO when transacting business on behalf of St Cross, the letters being taken to mean 'zu Osborne'. This charming story is however difficult to verify!

St Cross is a wonderfully tranquil place, hidden way from the teeming world all around it and remarkable for the fact that it is still delivering the charitable functions for which it was originally founded, nearly 900 years ago. Under Henry's original foundation the hospital was charged with providing 'a loaf of bread and a bottle of wine' to travellers; this has apparently been reduced over the years to 'a cup of beer and a piece of bread', today's equivalent of the dole which a visitor is said to be able to claim if they approach the caretaker! Meanwhile, in his book *England's Thousand Best Churches*, Simon Jenkins speculates that one of the periods when St Cross was beset by corruption and poverty may have inspired Trollope's book *The Warden*.

Romsey Abbey

Originally a Saxon nunnery a few miles North West of Southampton close to the river Test.

Look for arches in the nave which rise layer upon layer to the clerestory, the memorials to the Palmerston family and to Lord Mountbatten of Burma, the Saxon rood and the tower rising above the crossing.

Roughly fifteen miles west of St Cross is the abbey at Romsey, lying in the Test valley. Founded in 907 by Edward, the son of King Alfred, ruler of Wessex, the Benedictine abbey was established from the beginning as a Saxon nunnery. One of its first abbesses was Ethelflaeda or Elflaeda, Alfred's daughter. The church displays a board in the north aisle giving the names of all the abbesses who guided its fortunes from 959 to 1539, when the foundation was dissolved by Henry VIII's commissioners. The building was then sold to the people of Romsey for one hundred pounds, and was later used by them as their parish church.

The original wooden church began to be replaced by a more permanent stone structure from around 1000. In the early twelfth century the east end of the present Norman abbey was constructed, following which the arches towards the west end of the nave were finished about 1240. The nunnery was primarily intended as a place where the daughters of important people could be educated and at one point in the region of one hundred nuns came to be housed there.

The abbey has the proportions of a cathedral and dominates the surrounding land. Much change has taken place since the present church was built. Like many other buildings of its size and influence, Romsey experienced all the turmoil of medieval times, including the ravages of the Black Death which reduced the number of nuns to only nineteen. Later came the Reformation, when Henry VIII ordered the dissolution of the nunnery and the local Romsey people adjusted the structure to allow them to use it for their own purposes. The deed of sale signed by Henry VIII with his seal attached, is on display in the south choir aisle. A hundred years later, Cromwell's troops destroyed the organ and damaged much of the interior. The eighteenth century saw a period of stagnation when parts of the building housed a fire station and a local school, but in the next century considerable efforts were made to restore the church to its former status. Today, it is the largest parish church in Hampshire and ministers to a wide congregation from the town and the surrounding countryside.

Nearby Broadlands House, standing in 400 acres of parkland landscaped by 'Capability' Brown, has in recent years enjoyed close connections to the abbey. Two families which in their turn owned

Romsey Abbey.

Medieval image of an early Abbey.

Looking east.

The nave in late afternoon.

the Broadlands estate, are commemorated there. Lord Palmerston, Foreign Secretary and Prime Minister during some of Queen Victoria's reign, and members of his family are remembered in memorials beneath the west window; Lord Mountbatten of Burma, an Admiral of the Fleet and the last Viceroy of India, whose family lived at Broadlands more recently was buried in the south transept following his murder in 1979. The Mountbatten family pew is on the south side of the chancel.

The robust nature of the abbey's construction is very apparent. The external walls are massive, while the supporting piers underpin a high barrel roof. The stone used in building the Norman church came from the Isle of Wight and the nave arches are of Norman construction at the east end while those towards the west reflect the later Early English style. That stone was quarried at Chilmark, west of Salisbury. However, the abbey's most treasured possession is the Saxon rood or crucifix in St Anne's Chapel. It shows Christ on the cross with attendant angels and Roman soldiers and was possibly given to the nuns by King Edgar around 960. As the abbey guide comments 'It is remarkable to think that St Ethelflaeda herself would have known this rood'.

There are several chapels in the abbey commemorating local saints. The tower houses the bells which were removed from an earlier external bell tower in 1624 and placed in an octagon on the tower roof. The decorated Jacobean ceiling of the tower above the crossing provides the floor of the ringing chamber on top of it.

Romsey is a charming town and its abbey a place of great historical importance. It is close to the New Forest, an area enclosed by the early Norman kings to provide land across which they might hunt following the Conquest in 1066. William II died in the forest when he was struck by an arrow fired by Walter Tyrell and was later buried under the tower in Winchester Cathedral. In the New Forest are many reminders of the Norman era as well as Roman and Saxon times.

Chapter 3

South Dorset

▪ Lines closures by Beeching and their destiny fifty years later
▪ **Christchurch Priory** ▪ **Wimborne Minster** ▪

Getting There

Christchurch lies on the South Coast just to the east of Bournemouth and can be reached in an hour and fifty minutes on one of the regular South West semi-fast express services from London Waterloo to Poole.

Wimborne, situated about fifteen miles north-west of Bournemouth, no longer has a railway station. Those wishing to visit the Minster there should travel to Bournemouth and then take a bus or taxi to reach the town.

Railway Notes

To my mind, nothing scars our countryside so much as an abandoned railway route, particularly if the original construction included the building of great earthworks and elegantly fashioned bridges or viaducts. It always seems an insult to the memory of those who laboured so hard and long to build such structures, often only with rudimentary tools and under the most difficult and dangerous of conditions, that the results of their industry should later be so lightly discarded on the whim of a spurious economic argument or misguided judgement about their continued benefit. Man's ability to forecast the future has never been faultless and the logic of some decisions made by Dr Beeching in his report of the 1960s investigating the nation's future rail requirements, while at the time thought reasonable, have in many instances proved mistaken.

Almost half of Britain's rail network was earmarked for closure by Beeching but not all his recommendations were accepted by the government of the day. Some single line branches in, for example, rural areas like Norfolk or North East England did operate routes whose day had come. Hopelessly uneconomic and inefficient in their use of time and resources their passing went un-mourned by all but a few. Their replacement by local bus services proved relatively easy although ironically, many of these were later curtailed on economic grounds. Today, many of the abandoned routes have found a useful second career as long distance footpaths or cycle routes, thereby helping to encourage a significant surge in walking and cycling, the latter as either a means of transport or a recreational activity.

Overall, Beeching originally envisaged a truncated railway map leaving only a core of main lines; at one juncture no trains were to run north of Edinburgh or west of Exeter, while only principal centres of population were to remain connected to London. Local goods services were to be curtailed and replaced by road transport. The motor car and lorry were seen as king and the day of the train was over. But it didn't quite work out that way and the process for deciding closures soon became mired in controversy as communities fought to retain what were to them

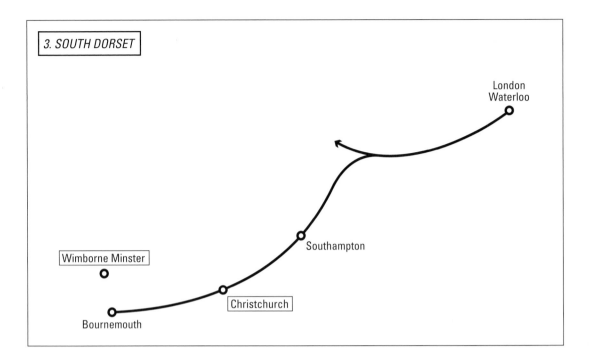

important local amenities. The resulting map of the network soon showed a different picture to that intended by Beeching; many lines were retained, his early draconian logic increasingly watered down by political argument. As might be expected in a democracy, debate reflecting all opinions eventually led to a series of pragmatic, if untidy, solutions.

The Settle to Carlisle Railway was threatened with closure on several occasions until finally reprieved in 1989. The South Western main line to Exeter via Salisbury was comprehensively downgraded, no doubt in the hope that it would eventual fail financially and could be closed. It took nearly forty years of innovative management to restore the line to the status of today's express route. Railways in every county were affected to some degree and conurbations also suffered closures. There was even a follow up plan, which would have seen the southern section of the former Great Central line from north of the Chilterns to London reduced to a series of feeder routes, its terminus in London, Marylebone Station, closed and converted to a bus depot. Today it is one of the most efficient and heavily used commuter routes into the capital.

Many abandoned lines still remain unused today other than by the occasional farmer to access his land. Some have been lost for ever, incorporated into road improvements – the Ripon bypass in North Yorkshire being an example – or housing schemes which have been allowed to sprawl across old tracks or to occupy redundant station land effectively blocking any chance of reinstatement. Notwithstanding, over the last twenty years an increasing programme of restoring routes to the benefit of local communities has taken place and more are on the agenda. The Sherwood Line in Nottinghamshire and the recently reopened Borders railway south of Edinburgh to Galashiels, are both examples of routes designed to provide better transport links and hence the prospect of greater economic potential for an area. More minor adjustments have taken place elsewhere, the impact of a short stretch of restored line or new alignment often conferring operational flexibility to an existing route out of proportion to the cost of the work.

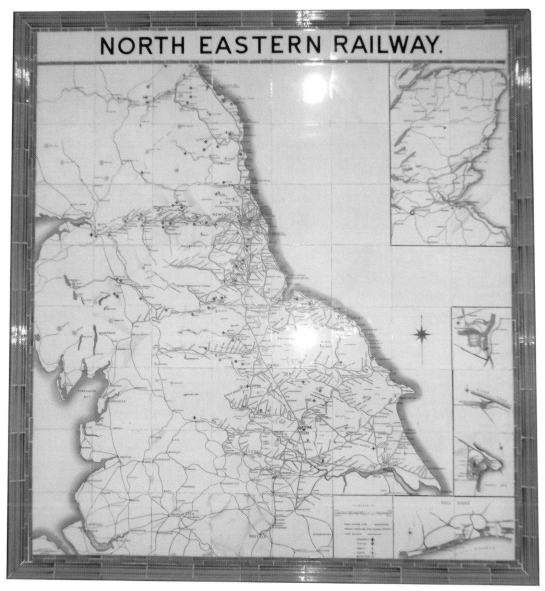

Map showing the proliferation of railway lines in North East England in the early twentieth century.

Was Beeching right? As with most questions of this nature – where politics heavily intrude – the answer will be a matter of opinion. He was undoubtedly right in the sense that a large number of lines and the size of the railway estate generally could no longer be justified in the post steam age; however some of his proposals went further than was necessary and had harmful effects, not realised at the time. The balance is now being redressed and many routes are once again fulfilling the purpose for which they were originally built nearly two hundred years ago, while other uses are gradually being found for those former lines which will never again see a train.

Christchurch Priory

One of England's less well known but great churches.

Look for the Norman pillars, the reredos behind the High Altar, the Salisbury Chantry and try to find the 'miraculous beam' and the misericords in the quire.

The 900 year old priory is another church with the proportions of a cathedral, being one of the longest parish churches in England. It stands on the edge of the town close to the river Avon but is not the first church to be built in Christchurch; that was a Saxon church probably constructed in the seventh century. In the eleventh century, Ranulf Flambard, principal minister to William II and later Bishop of Durham, instructed that the Saxon church be demolished and a Norman priory constructed in its place. The resulting lofty nave and transepts are built in the Norman style with massive pillars and rounded arches with the quire and Lady Chapel being added thereafter, generally reflecting the later Perpendicular style. The building, originally part of an Augustinian monastery, was begun in 1094. Christchurch suffered little at the time of the Reformation although the monastic buildings were damaged and the status of 'priory' lost.

The Priory.

Jane Gray's 900 year commemoration window.

The High altar and reredos.

A window in the north transept, created by Jane Gray in 1994, commemorates the church's 900 years. Against the background of a starry night it shows a cross, surrounded by circles, intended by the creator to represent eternity and perfection thereby creating a feeling of space and time. The centre of the largest circle contains the letters Chi-Ro, the monogram of Christ, thereby demonstrating and reaffirming 900 years of Christian worship at Christchurch.

Behind the high altar is the reredos which depicts the relationship between Jesse and Christ through the forty-three generations which separated them. Above is a mural showing the risen Christ painted by Hans Feibusch in 1967. East of the high altar and beyond the screen is the Lady Chapel with its striking window behind the altar. The central tower collapsed in the fifteenth century and was replaced by the west tower of today's church.

High up on the south side of the entrance to the Lady Chapel, protruding from an arch, is the 'miraculous beam'. Legend has it that, following a disagreement as to where Ranulf Flambard should build his church and after the present site was chosen, a series of curious incidents took place during construction. One story suggests that an internal wooden beam was cut too short but, left overnight to be substituted next day, it was miraculously found in the morning to be in position and of the correct length. Another anecdote suggests the presence of a mysterious

The Salisbury Chantry.

carpenter who worked throughout construction but who was never present at meals or when the workmen were paid. Could this have been the carpenter Jesus Christ?

The church contains a number of chantries. These chapels were built in many churches and cathedrals in medieval times as places of prayer for the souls of former bishops or important people to celebrate their lives and speed their way to Heaven; many have since been removed although some of the more ornate are preserved in various of the larger churches.

In the north quire aisle is the Salisbury chantry, built during the Tudor period around 1529. It is constructed of Caen stone from France and commemorates Margaret Pole, Countess of Salisbury and the only woman in the sixteenth century to hold a peerage in her own right. She was a lady in waiting to Anne Boleyn, second wife of Henry VIII. Inevitably given the extraordinary circumstances of that time she became caught up in the intrigues and turmoil of life at court. Her eldest son Reginald, at one time Dean of Wimborne, denounced Henry VIII for his plans to reform the monasteries and eventually Margaret Pole herself fell foul of the king. She was arraigned for treason and condemned to death, her execution taking place on Tower Green on 27 May 1541. She was a proud woman and refused to kneel and put her head on the block, stipulating that she should instead be decapitated standing upright. This unconventional approach was further complicated by the fact that the regular executioner was absent and his inexperienced deputy had to perform the task of taking her life. It took eleven blows with a sword before she eventually died.

Margaret Pole had four sons, one of them – Reginald - being the last Roman Catholic Archbishop of Canterbury under Queen Mary. On her death in 1558, Mary was succeeded by Elizabeth, during whose reign England moved inexorably towards becoming a Protestant country, obedience to the Pope being finally abandoned.

On the north side of the chancel opposite the 'miraculous beam' is the entrance to St Michael's Loft Museum, originally a school for monks and later a grammar school; it is situated above the Lady Chapel and can be reached by ascending a staircase. Today it tells the visitor about the life of the Priory.

Christchurch may be off the beaten track and be time-consuming to reach. However, it is well worth the journey and a visit will tell you much about life in the years before and after the Reformation. It is said that the last prior, John Draper, had the unenviable task of surrendering the Priory and its riches to the commissioners sent by Henry VIII. Draper has a chantry at the east end of the church, fitting recognition no doubt of the way in which he discharged his final duties, thereby ensuring that Christchurch Priory escaped relatively unscathed from the turbulence of the Reformation years.

Wimborne Minster

Still styled a minster Wimborne has a long and fascinating history.

Look for the astronomical clock, the royal coat of arms above the nave, the Ettricke tomb and the Grenadier quarter jack high up on the north side of the west tower.

The word 'minster' is used to describe a church which, in Anglo Saxon times, was a missionary centre, a place from which the clergy would go out into surrounding areas to apprise people about God and the teachings of the bible. A church of any size could be a minster and indeed both cathedrals and tiny churches often enjoyed such an appellation. Today, the title is used less often, although the cathedrals at York and Southwell still style themselves minsters as do a number of parish churches. Wimborne is one of them and the town takes its name as a result.

St Cuthburga founded a Benedictine nunnery in Wimborne around 705. At its peak, the nunnery may have housed as many as 500 nuns before it was burnt by the Vikings during one of their raids on Wessex in 1013. The nunnery was never rebuilt and little evidence of it is to be seen today. In 1043, Edward the Confessor inaugurated a new order of secular, non-monastic monks on the site and during the eleventh century most of today's church was built by the Normans. Interestingly, in 1318 Edward II declared the church to be a Royal Peculiar, which absolved it from diocesan control. Today the term is used to describe those churches directly under the authority of the Crown, such as Westminster Abbey and St George's Chapel, Windsor. At Wimborne, the Royal Peculiar was repealed in 1846 and today the church is overseen by twelve governors who, *inter alia*, choose the rector.

The minster is notable for its two towers. That in the centre dates from the late twelfth century and its foundations may contain remnants of the Saxon church. The Perpendicular western tower

The central tower.

was constructed around 1464 to house the bells which are still rung from a chamber above the baptistry. The minster guide records that for several years after completion the tower suffered from instability; in 1548 the west door had to be bricked up to forestall possible collapse while in 1664 the churchwardens recorded 'paying in beere to the ringers for a peele to try if the tower shook – one shilling.' By the end of the nineteenth century the west tower had finally been made safe.

High up on the south side of the baptistry is a fourteenth century astronomical clock, the casing Elizabethan but the face and dial much older. The clock was redecorated in 1979. Below it hang two leather water buckets, a reminder that once the firefighting resources of a parish were

The nave looking west.

often kept in the church tower. A tomb stone on the opposite wall records the life of Gulliver, a well-known Dorset smuggler who always managed to keep ahead of the law despite many narrow escapes. The church guide comments that 'it says much for public opinion at the time that he eventually became a respected resident of Wimborne'.

The fourteenth-century astronomical clock.

The difference in style of the arches in the nave is very marked; the two westernmost were built in the decorated style while the three further east are Norman. They are decorated with chevron patterns and corbel figures of humans and animals. There are a further two Norman arches adjacent to the central tower which are older than the rest. At the west end of the nave and high up on the wall is a royal coat of arms; Wimborne suffered little damage during the Civil War but after Charles I's execution the arms were painted out only to be speedily restored when Charles II was restored to the throne.

The Ettricke 'man in the wall' tomb.

There are a number of chapels at the east end. Holy Trinity Chapel contains the burial place of Anthony Ettricke, a barrister who was Recorder of Poole for twenty years in the latter half of the seventeenth century. In 1685 he committed the Duke of Monmouth for trial charged with rebellion, the latter having been found hiding beneath an ash tree in the vicinity; a week after his arrest Monmouth was beheaded. Ettricke seems to have had a love-hate relationship with the people of Wimborne; at one moment he allowed himself to be offended by their attitudes and solemnly declared that 'he would never be buried within the church or without it – neither below ground nor above it'. Later, having overcome his pique and wishing to be buried with his ancestors but not wishing to break his original oath, he gained permission to hollow out a recess in a chapel wall where his coffin was to be placed. So convinced was he that he would die in 1693, he inscribed the date on his coffin; in fact he lived until 1703.

There is much to see in the vicinity of the quire and the presbytery: the charming crypt, built in 1340, beneath the presbytery and reached by stairs; the east window containing part of a Jesse window of fifteenth century Belgian glass; the tomb of John Beaufort and his wife, grandparents of Henry VII near the high altar and the chained library above the quire vestry all reward a visit. The library with its collection of ancient tomes has been described as 'almost a miniature of Hereford', a reference to the magnificent chained library in the cathedral there. Some of the seventeenth century quire stalls

The central and western towers.

The Grenadier 'quarter jack'.

have carved misericords, that closest to the Rector's stall being a remarkably fine image of a green man. Green men were originally a pagan symbol, later adopted by Christians. They take the form of a detached head surrounded by 'green' twigs and branches, some growing out of the head's various orifices. They associate humans with trees and are thought to symbolise rebirth. They are not usually green in colour. They can be found in many churches and public buildings and are widespread on the Continent as they are in England.

Misericords too can be found in the stalls of many churches. Literally translated as 'mercy seats' they take the form of a tip up seat hinged at its base. In medieval times when monks had to stand for long periods and would often tire,

Green Man – An embroidered depiction of a 'Green Man'.
(Mrs R.G.Naylor)

Wimborne Minster west window.

they allowed the occupant of a stall to perch, thereby surreptitiously resting his limbs. The seats are invariably carved with images of people or animals and several examples are mentioned in this book.

Outside the minster on the north side of the west tower is the Quarter Jack: originally the figure of a monk carved in 1612 by a Blandford craftsman for ten shillings, he was replaced by a Grenadier at the time of the Napoleonic wars. He strikes two bells every quarter hour. On the south side of the tower is a sundial with three faces thereby allowing the time to be told throughout the day. It was originally part of the south transept end wall but was moved to its present position in 1891.

Visiting Wimborne Minster on a bright September morning was a joy, doubly so since throughout my time in the church a piano in the nave was being played by a volunteer. Her rendering of the music added to the delight of discovering the minster's treasures.

Chapter 4

North Dorset

■ The carriage of passengers ■ **Sherborne Abbey**
■ **Milton Abbey** ■

Getting There

Sherborne is situated on the former London and South Western Railway (LSWR) main line to Exeter. This is the second of two routes which connect the capital with Exeter and the West Country. From Waterloo the journey to Sherborne takes two hours, with a further hour to Exeter.

Milton Abbey cannot be reached directly by train, there being no railway station within twenty-five miles. A traveller should therefore travel either to Sherborne or Poole (on the Weymouth line from Waterloo) and take a taxi or bus, although there are unfortunately few of the latter.

Railway Notes

Such was the novelty of train travel in the earliest days of the railways that little thought was given to the comfort of passengers or indeed their safety. The first wagons conveying people were open to the elements and seating was not provided except in vehicles set aside for the more important in society, who might be accommodated in a stage coach chassis placed upon a flat railway wagon. Conceptually, the early carriage of passengers by train was seen as an extension of stage coach travel, the locomotive being seen by some as simply a replacement for the horse.

Over the last two centuries standards of safety and comfort have developed, although maybe not as quickly as some would have wished. Today, passengers in first class can expect a reasonable level of luxury although it may cost them dear in fares. Standard class accommodation too has improved, although the satisfaction of a journey by train in modern, better equipped carriages can often lose its appeal when services become overcrowded and there is little space to store luggage. In a very real sense travel by rail has become a victim of its own success, as increasing numbers opt to use the train rather than go by air or road. In parallel, there has only recently been speculation in the transport media about the prospect of a future decline in car ownership, mainly brought about by the inadequacy of the national road system leading to a wish to find alternative and better means of personal transport.

During the twentieth century, thought was given to the different ways in which trains might provide additional or more innovative ways to accommodate the needs of the passenger. For instance, slip coaches were first introduced in 1858 by railways in the South of England, thereby allowing additional stations to be called at without increasing journey times. By decoupling the last coach or coaches of a train while it was still in motion a portion could be detached and used to serve a station without the need to stop the main train. Once separation from the parent train had taken place, the detached portion would freewheel into the platform, controlled by a guard who would use the

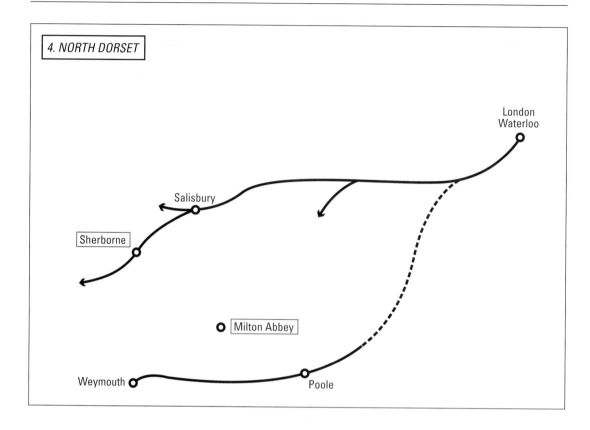

4. NORTH DORSET

London
Waterloo

Salisbury

Sherborne

Milton Abbey

Weymouth

Poole

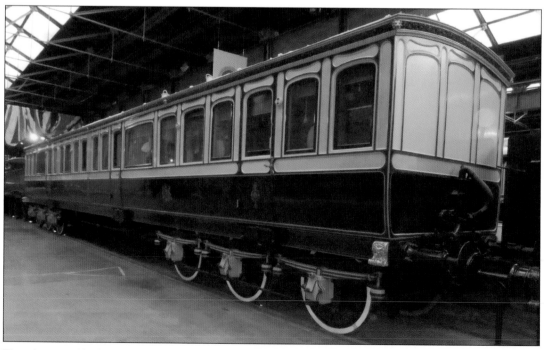

The saloon used by Queen Victoria in the latter years of the nineteenth century, principally for journeys to Scotland.

A Midland Railway third class dining car operating on routes to Scotland 1910 to 1950.

An overnight train conveying sleeping car passengers from Inverness to London.

The interior of a sleeping compartment set out for standard class occupation. (Colin J Marsden)

carriages' own braking system, to bring them to a stop at the required spot. There was of course no similar system to reconnect a 'slipped' coach to its train and a stop always had to be made for passengers to be picked up. The last slip carriage was used at Bicester in 1960 on the GWR route from Paddington to Birmingham. However there is no record suggesting how passengers viewed the experience of being delivered to their destination in such a manner!

Other innovations of early railways were sleeping and restaurant cars. Both made their first appearance in the 1870s and added greatly to the convenience of long distance travel. To be able to journey overnight from London to Edinburgh saved time and money, while being served a hot meal en route could add to the convenience and pleasure of a journey. Sleeping cars continue in use on routes over 300 miles or more and are as well patronised as ever, but sadly, other than on a very limited number of trains, restaurant cars have virtually disappeared, being replaced by the buffet car or catering trolley. Unlike Continental express trains which tend to cover longer distances in a single journey, the average British journey does not justify the use of such amenities, especially in an age when the economics of services are kept under continual review. While it might be tempting to talk about a renaissance in travel by rail today, such are the different circumstances of the country that there can be no going back to the early twentieth century which was truly the age of the train.

However, not everything has been reduced to the level of a basic service and fresh ideas for making journeys both a pleasure and a convenience are emerging all the time. Building on the thinking already developed by some private companies in combining travel and visits to historic places or scenic parts of Britain, the running of publicly provided 'tourist' services in some areas might soon be developed by operating companies. Journeys over the Pennines along the Settle to Carlisle line or over some routes in the Highlands of Scotland could in the future see the introduction of carriages with wide vista windows or observation cars to attract the leisure traveller. Meanwhile, there is even a chance that in time the daily grind of the long suffering commuter may be alleviated if double deck carriages are introduced on suitable suburban lines to create additional seating. While much will depend upon the ability to re-engineer the loading gauge to provide the necessary clearances in tunnels or at bridges such measures could make a very significant difference to standards of travel and passenger comfort. Plans to run a limited number of double deck suburban trains on the Waterloo to Southampton route could soon be under discussion and could materialise in the next few years. Meanwhile double decking was tried by the Southern Railway in the early 1950s but later abandoned, mainly because of the delays which arose when passengers boarded and the cramped internal layout of the carriages.

A forerunner of things to come in Britain? A double deck suburban commuter train operating in Toronto, Canada. (Colin J Marsden).

Sherborne Abbey

An abbey which celebrates thirteen centuries of history and which has one of the oldest and finest vaulted roofs in England.

Look for the two baptismal fonts, the reddened walls of the quire and tower, the misericords in the quire and the glass reredos in the Lady Chapel.

The diocese of Sherborne was created in 705 when responsibility for the western part of the Winchester diocese was transferred there; the first Bishop of the West Saxons was Aldhem. The cathedral served him and his twenty-six successors until 1075 when, following the Norman Conquest, the bishop's seat was moved to Old Sarum and later to Salisbury where it remains to this day. Today there is still a Bishop of Sherborne but he is a suffragan to Salisbury and has no seat or throne of his own.

A Benedictine Abbey was established in 998 and remained until the Dissolution in the sixteenth century, since when it has been the local parish church. Built of Ham stone, the abbey stands in the centre of the town surrounded by buildings of similar materials. It is an imposing structure, both when viewed from outside but even more so once entered. The pillars of the nave and quire run the length of the building, rising to meld into a fine fan vaulted roof, one of the oldest and most magnificent in England. Studded with a number of bosses, the simplicity of the roof design and the uncluttered nature of the nave make the abbey an easy and pleasant building to absorb. Collins *Guide to English Parish Churches* describes 'the vaults of the nave and the quire as among the finest in existence'.

Two of Alfred the Great's brothers are thought to be buried at Sherborne - Ethelbald and Ethelbert – both being kings of Wessex in their time. Centuries later, Sir Walter Raleigh worshipped

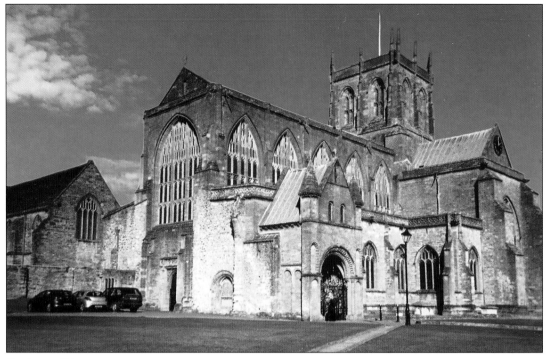

Sherborne Abbey.

in the church. During the time that the abbey was used by the Benedictines, a small church was added at the west end to enable the local people to worship without entering the abbey proper. The 'joins' where the two structures met before the smaller church was demolished can still be seen. However this segregation caused friction, local people resenting being excluded from what had been their church, and in 1437 matters took an ugly turn when they built their own baptismal font rather than seek the abbot's permission every time they wanted to use that in the abbey. The immediate response from the abbot was to order the destruction of the newly built font which led to a riot, followed by a fire in the quire and at the tower crossing. Fire damage explains why areas of the abbey still have reddened walls in various places. The dispute was eventually settled by the Pope, the local people having to pay for the damage, although they got their revenge a hundred years later when the abbey was repossessed following the Dissolution. One of their first acts was to dismantle their church at the west end.

There are two fonts in the building; that in the Bow Chapel, may contain some remnants of the font smashed on the orders of the abbot in 1437. The great west window was created by John Hayward and dedicated in the presence of Elizabeth II in 1998. Moving east to the quire, the visitor will see a number of medieval misericords in the rear stalls. From the quire, entrance can be gained to a number of chapels, principal among them the Lady Chapel with its engraved glass reredos by Lawrence Whistler and the Bow Chapel which used at one time to be the headmaster's study when nearby Sherborne School had closer links to the abbey. Meanwhile, the great east window is mid nineteenth century and features the apostles Matthew, Mark, Luke and John and local saints Sidwell and Juthware. Nearby in the Wykeham Chapel is a monument to Sir John Horsey, who purchased the abbey estate lands at the time of the Dissolution.

Milton Abbey

A fourteenth century abbey, later rebuilt without a nave following a fire and set in wonderful surroundings.

Look for the Pugin window in the south transept and the memorials to the Tregonwell and Damer families.

As recorded at the head of this chapter Milton Abbey lies in the depths of the Dorset countryside and is not readily accessible by public transport; the best way to reach it and to see something of the beautiful surrounding countryside is to hire a car at the nearest convenient railway station.

A church was founded at Milton by King Athelstan in 937 and in 964 Benedictine monks from Glastonbury were installed there. In 1309, a lightning strike led to a fire which burnt down most of the building. When rebuilt, only the east end as far as the crossing was restored and the truncated building therefore has no nave. Following the Dissolution, the abbey estate was purchased by Sir John Tregonwell, who had been of assistance to Henry VIII in arranging his divorce from Catherine of Aragon in 1533.

Two hundred years later, Joseph Damer, later created Earl of Dorchester, demolished the surrounding buildings of the abbey and built a large mansion. It is this sequence of events which has led to this most interesting of buildings to be now standing in the depths of the Dorset countryside, remote from civilisation and seemingly unloved. .

Today the abbey stands next to the mansion and a group of more recent buildings, all of which now house Milton Abbey School, a public school which bought the estate in 1953. The views from the campus are breathtaking, rolling hills interspersed with shallow, wooded valleys with

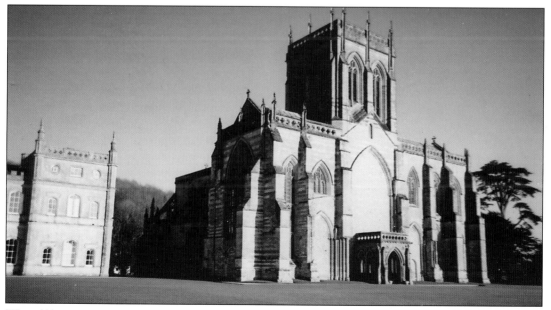

Milton Abbey.

hardly a house in sight. This landscape was created by Lancelot 'Capability' Brown in 1763 on the instructions of Joseph Damer, who wanted a suitable design for his new house. In the process a new 'model' village was established a mile away; the resulting scene must provide one of the finest settings for any church in England.

The interior of the abbey is fourteenth century Perpendicular and is constructed in Ham and Chilmark stone. The roof is covered in lierne vaults, a design where the shorter ribs in the vaulting create intricate patterns by connecting between the longer ribs rather than to a boss. Lierne vaulting can be found in the cathedrals at Bristol and Ely and in churches elsewhere. Meanwhile at Milton there is a *pulpitum* screen, on the east side of which are panel paintings of Athelstan and his mother. There are few memorials and the building presents a rather soulless appearance until explored. In the north transept is a memorial to the Damers, creators of the setting, with a tomb designed by Robert Adam, while in the south aisle is a memorial to the Tregonwell family; an explanatory notice relates the story of Sir John Tregonwell bequeathing his library to the church in gratitude for his escape from death when as a child he fell from the abbey roof, apparently being saved by his breeches filling with air and acting as a parachute to slow his descent!

Most of the glass is clear, although the window in the south transept merits special attention. It depicts a tree of Jesse, recording Christ's lineage , and was designed by Augustus Pugin in 1847.

Painted in vivid colours, it and its counterpart in the north transept are exceptionally tall. Pugin, born in 1812, lived only forty years but during his life designed many buildings and decorated their interiors, including in the Houses of Parliament. He was a leading member of the Gothic Revival movement which reached its peak in the nineteenth century; advocates of the movement sought to revive the architecture of the Gothic period of the twelfth to sixteenth centuries and the movement came to be associated with an awakening of High Church or Anglo Catholic beliefs.

In 1852, the Hambro family purchased the estate and commissioned George Gilbert Scott to undertake certain restoration work within the abbey. In 1932, the Ecclesiastical Commission bought the abbey and surrounding buildings, the latter being sold to the school in 1957.

Despite the remoteness of its location and its inaccessibility by public transport, Milton Abbey will reward any visit, if only for the sheer joy of seeing the abbey building in such a magnificent rural setting. John Betjeman in Collins *Guide to English Parish Churches* describes Milton Abbey 'as the most impressive church in Dorset'.

Pugin's south transept window.

South West

Bath Abbey.

The tower, St. Andrew's Church, Cullompton.

Chapter 5

Devon

■ A train driver's responsibilities ■ **Church of the Holy Cross, Crediton**
■ **St Andrew's Church, Cullompton** ■ Dawlish 2014 ■

Getting There

A fast train from London Paddington to Tiverton Parkway takes approximately two hours and ten minutes. However not all trains stop at Tiverton and a change may be necessary at Taunton. Cullompton is ten minutes by taxi from Tiverton station.

Crediton can be reached by train from Paddington via Exeter (St David's) on the same line. Journey time is just over two hours. Change at Exeter into a local Barnstaple train which will take approximately ten minutes to reach Crediton.

Railway Notes

The responsibilities placed upon those who drive trains will be self-evident. Ever since the earliest days of steam power, the safety of passengers as laid down in the 'rule book', has been their foremost priority. Extensive training and strict compliance with the regulations which govern the operation of railways have always been essential and remain so. Two hundred years later, that responsibility is no less onerous but today the assistance provided to drivers in the form of control systems and computers, programmed to govern speed and react to potential problems on a route, makes the job more comfortable but no less demanding. Training is also more comprehensive.

Engine drivers in the steam age were men of enormous stature and experience, held in great respect by their peers, who only achieved the right to drive express services after many years spent working their way up through the ranks of the industry. Those who reached the highest levels of their profession – known as the 'top link' – would have spent years cleaning engines in locomotive depots before being passed to become stokers, employed to shovel coal and tend certain aspects of the locomotive's running when hauling a train. After a period in that job, a fireman would be promoted to drive local trains or freight services before being allowed to handle the fastest expresses. Such a progression might take forty years or more and relied to a great extent upon experience gained from working with more experienced colleagues.

The pressure placed upon a steam locomotive driver was both physically and mentally demanding. Shifts were long and the preparation of an engine before a journey required considerable time checking all aspects of its operation. A driver needed to know every detail of the route he was to drive, speed restrictions and any temporary control measures as well as the braking distance of his train, its timetable and the position of line-side signals regulating its progress. There were few devices to help him – speedometers were not fitted for many years and the first automatic train control systems did not appear until between the wars – while

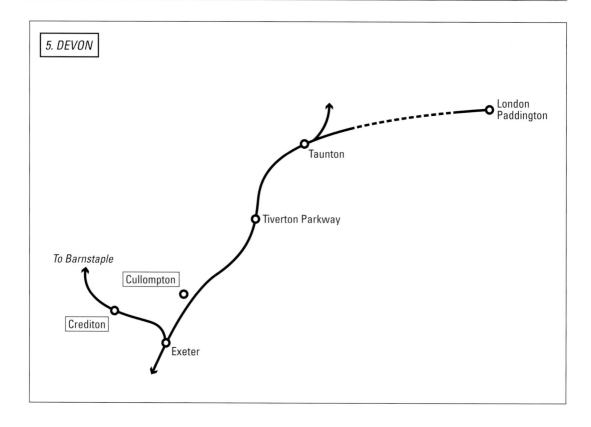

5. DEVON

London
Paddington

Taunton

Tiverton Parkway

To Barnstaple

Cullompton

Crediton

Exeter

strict attention to signals meant that a driver spent much of a journey in all weathers peering ahead to see if his route was clear. However, his prime task, apart from ensuring the safety of his train, was, in concert with his fireman, to ensure that his engine maintained sufficient steam to haul its train to its destination on time and using only the minimum resources of coal and water.

The stress placed upon even the most experienced drivers could lead to unfortunate accidents. A good example of how a momentary lapse could bring disaster occurred at Norton Fitzwarren, a few miles west of Taunton, in the early hours of 4 November 1940 when the overnight sleeping car train to Penzance was diverted from its usual route due to late running and in order to allow a second train, carrying newspapers, to overtake it. Both trains had passed through Taunton within minutes of each other but the driver of the sleeper failed to appreciate that, after leaving the station, his train had been routed onto the relief line rather than, as more usually, taking the fast line westwards. It was not until he was overtaken by the newspaper train travelling on the parallel main line and only some 400 yards before the two tracks merged into one at Norton Fitzwarren, that he realised his error. Seconds later the locomotive and first six coaches of the sleeper crashed through catch points designed to protect the junction of the two lines, resulting in half the sleeper train being spread-eagled across all lines. Twenty seven people were killed and many others of the 900 passengers hurt. This accident on a dark night and in wartime when the black out and enemy aerial action added to the difficulties, arose because an experienced driver suffered a momentary lapse; he assumed that his train was on the route that it would normally have taken after leaving Taunton and was unaware of the

A top link locomotive driver of the 1930s. [SSPL]

The Driver of the overnight Inverness to London sleeper train 2015.

decision to divert it to allow priority to be given to the newspaper train. His uncharacteristic error resulted in terrible consequences. Modern safety devices would almost certainly have prevented such a disaster; today the passage of trains is so closely controlled that travel by rail is seen as one of the safest means of transport, if not the safest.

The Church of the Holy Cross, Crediton

A church site the origins of which go back to Saxon times. Once a cathedral, the present day church is of similar proportions.

Look for the window commemorating St Boniface, the Buller memorial, the Norman font and the Governors' room.

The reader may wonder why the churches at Crediton and Cullompton, neither of which are today abbeys or priories, should be included in this book. However both have interesting backgrounds – especially Crediton – and were in the past seemingly centres of considerable religious importance and influence. The history of the two churches helps to tell us, not only about how Christianity developed locally, but also gives an indication how the Church in general has adapted to the many changes forced upon it throughout history.

The first church to be built at Crediton was probably a Saxon place of worship and is believed to have been associated with St Boniface (original name Wynfrith) who was born in the area in the last quarter of the seventh century. Whether a monastery was actually built by him at Crediton at that time is unclear but Boniface, a recognised Christian missionary, gained in stature when he travelled to the country we now know as Germany in his efforts to convert pagan people there to Christianity. He was so successful, establishing new churches, revitalising others and gaining converts, that he was created an archbishop by the Pope. He died in 754 when he and his followers

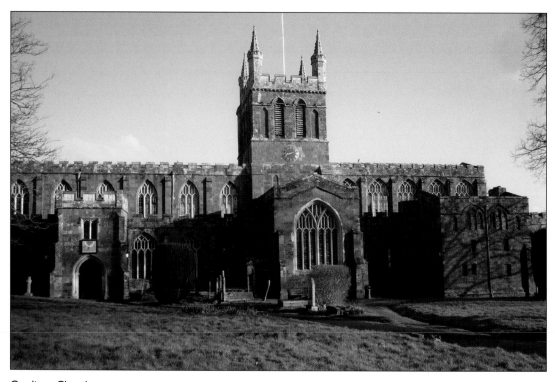

Crediton Church.

The Buller memorial.

were attacked by a hostile band; Boniface allegedly held up his bible in the face of his enemies, the sword of one impaling the book. Consequently the image of Boniface holding a book run through by a sword can be seen in many churches associated with the saint, including in the south-west aisle at Crediton.

Since Boniface's time there have been at least four churches on the site in Crediton. In the tenth century, the diocese of Sherborne in Dorset was divided and Crediton became the centre of a new diocese to the west with Eadulf as the first bishop. Thereafter a new cathedral was built, probably constructed in wood, and nine bishops subsequently ministered to the needs of the people until, in 1050, the then bishop, Leofric, proposed that the see be moved to Exeter where he was enthroned in the presence of Edward the Confessor. Crediton then became a collegiate church and was rebuilt in stone. The Bishop of Crediton is today a suffragan of Exeter but, like his colleague at Sherborne, does not have a seat or throne in the church from which he takes his title.

The church was developed in the thirteenth century when a Lady Chapel and Chapter House were built. However, in the fifteenth century rebuilding became necessary and as a result of that work, begun in 1409, the present Perpendicular church took shape. In 1545, following the Dissolution of the Monasteries by Henry VIII, Crediton's position as a College of Clergy ended. Local people then purchased the building and Edward VI granted a charter authorising a corporation of twelve governors to administer the church, its lands and its tithes and to establish a grammar school, located in the Lady Chapel. The governors were to be – and remain – independent of the local bishop in secular matters.

Today's church is built of red sandstone quarried locally and is 230 feet in length, much longer than the average parish church. In keeping with its past role as a cathedral, it has a chancel, quire, nave, a tower – the oldest part of the church – transepts, side aisles, a Lady Chapel and originally a Chapter House. In 1848 the governors ordered a series of renovations which were undertaken under the direction of John Hayward, a distinguished Exeter architect. Included were the restoration of the Lady Chapel, the grammar school having moved elsewhere, the elevation of the high altar and the rebuilding of the roof.

There is much to see in the church including a Norman baptismal font, a three-seat sedilia or priests' seats to the south of the high altar which shows signs of damage probably sustained during the Reformation period and a fine sun dial above the porch into the south aisle. However, dominating the interior of the church is a memorial to General Sir Redvers Buller, a local man who commanded an Army Corps during the Boer War at the end of the nineteenth century when he led the relief of Ladysmith. He had won a Victoria Cross during the previous Zulu wars when, in 1879, he displayed great bravery in rescuing three soldiers. However, despite his becoming a controversial figure with his military competence later questioned in some quarters, he clearly commanded the affections of the people of this part of Devon and was rewarded with a larger-than-life memorial. John Betjeman in the Collins *Guide to English Parish Churches* he edited, comments 'Unfortunate memorial by Caroe above the chancel arch to Sir Redvers Buller, who was vastly admired by Devonians if not by the outside world'.

St Andrew's Church, Cullompton

A brightly decorated church with several unique features and a history which reflects the many changes undergone by religious communities over the centuries.

Look for the 'wagon' roof – the four headed bosses – the brightly painted screen – Lane's aisle and the Golgotha timbers. If you are allowed to, climb the church tower and view the lovely Exe valley.

Built in the English Perpendicular style during the fifteenth century this is a most enjoyable church to visit with its intricate 'wagon' roof and brightly painted screen. Indeed, I chose it for inclusion because its vivid and welcoming ambience made it seem rather special. The tower, built in the middle 1540s, is typical of so many Devon churches and gives unparalleled views across the river Exe valley. John Betjeman comments that 'the.fine red tower is one of the things one looks for from the Western Region expresses dashing down to Exeter'.

There were originally murals on the walls of the side aisles, one reputedly showing St Christopher, nine feet high with Christ on his shoulders, but across the centuries they have been covered and uncovered several times depending upon the mood of the times. The first attempt to obliterate them probably took place during the Reformation, while at the end of the eighteenth century the then vicar insisted they once more be covered 'lest they distract the attention of the congregation'. In 1947, the debate over whether they should be uncovered or not was finally brought to an end when 'their restoration was agreed to be out of the question' by the Royal College of Art.

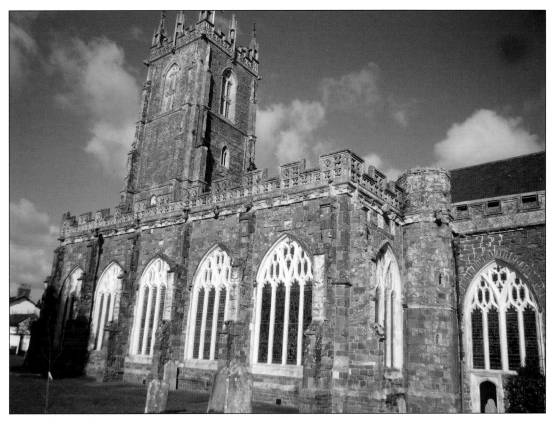

St. Andrew's Church, Cullompton.

There is a profusion of roof bosses above the nave and chancel, some rather faded but others more decipherable, with nine of them showing four faces combined in a single boss. Lane's aisle on the south side of the church was built between 1525 and 1530 and commemorates John Lane, a local cloth merchant who established a successful overseas trade, depicted in images of shears and the ships which carried his products across the oceans. The stone aisle roof is fan vaulted, in contrast to the wooden roof of the nave. It is possible that the aisle may have been intended as Lane's chantry chapel, its added embellishment over several generations being the result of rivalry with another local family, the Moores, who had their own chapel on the north side of the church.

At the west end of Lane's aisle are two large baulks of oak carved to show rocks covered with skulls and bones. Called the Golgotha these timber beams were originally the base of a cross which would have been placed on top of the rood screen, presumably to remind worshippers of the Crucifixion. Speculation has it that the structure was removed in the reign of Edward VI when, as part of the continuing programme of change, the wall murals were also once more covered over. The Golgotha is thought to be unique in England if not in Christendom. The timber is now five hundred years old and gives the appearance of being as hard as stone.

The early years of the nineteenth century were difficult times across the nation – the aftermath of the Napoleonic wars, the passing of the Corn Laws leading to social unrest in towns and the intensification of the industrial revolution – and never more so than at Cullompton, where the fabric

The decorated screen.

The Golgotha.

of the church fell into disrepair and disputes occurred within the parish. However, a benefactor appeared in the shape of William Froude, the civil engineer responsible for building Brunel's Great Western Railway from Taunton to Exeter who was residing temporarily in the town. Fearful that the passage of trains so close to the church might further damage the fabric, in the early 1840s Froude arranged, and to a large extent paid for, the renovation of the chancel and its roof and the enlargement of the east window. He also offered to do similar work on the nave if the people of Cullompton paid a tenth of the cost, something they refused. In 1844, the line was completed and Froude moved elsewhere, sadly the church being left with an un-refurbished nave roof.

In the north east side of Moores Chapel hangs a Stars and Stripes flag with a descriptive board recording that in November 1943 a service was held to give thanks for the arrival and presence of American troops in the area prior to the D Day landings; the names of all present are listed, the service fitting testimony to the friendship and gratitude shown to the billeted troops by local people at a time of great peril for the free world.

Railway Notes

Ever since its construction by Brunel in the 1840s, the Great Western main line from Exeter to Cornwall has been subject to interruption by adverse weather causing train movements to be suspended to avoid danger to life. The line between Exeter and Newton Abbot runs close to the sea wall in several places and when storms blow up in the English Channel, they can hit the coast with considerable ferocity. On 4 and 5 February 2014, strong winds and high seas wrought considerable damage causing the sea wall to be breached and sections of the railway line to collapse.

As a result of the February storm, a hundred metres of line were washed away and Dawlish Station was damaged. An army of 300 Network Rail engineers, supported by contractors, was drafted in to rebuild the line as soon as weather conditions permitted; this work included positioning shipping containers to provide a temporary sea wall, then rebuilding Brunel's original sea defences, relaying track and installing new signalling systems and rebuilding much of Dawlish Station. In addition, four miles of adjoining track close to the sea had to be cleared and in places repaired, while an area of collapsed cliff face in Teignmouth needed to be removed and the site stabilised to prevent future obstruction. In total, 6,000 tonnes of concrete and 150 tonnes of steel were used and trains were unable to run for two months. It is greatly to the credit of those responsible in Network Rail that the line was restored so quickly, enabling local communities to once again be connected to the outside world.

The fragility of the rail link along this stretch of the coast has been a concern for years, for both railway engineers and the travelling public. People living to the west of Dawlish have long worried about the resilience of a rail link upon which so many depend. Historically, there used to be two routes to Plymouth from Exeter; the Great Western route built along the coast to Newton Abbot and across South Devon, while the former Southern Railway followed an inland alignment west of Dartmoor to Plymouth. This latter route was closed following the Beeching proposals in the late 1960s, although much of the track bed of the line remains in place and could now be reinstated. Other shorter routes, designed to by-pass the area threatened by the sea have been identified, including a route first planned in 1935 which would have diverted the line inland between Exminster and Newton Abbot; this undeveloped route, known as the Dawlish Avoiding Line, was apparently guaranteed government funding at that time and some survey work took place but all work was halted on the outbreak of the Second World War, never to be resumed.

How the problems of guaranteeing rail links to the South West will eventually be achieved remains to be seen. Cost will be crucial but the aspirations and interests of those living around Torbay and further west towards Plymouth and beyond will play an important part in deciding the best option. Politically, the issue is unlikely to go away, a problem – first envisaged by Brunel over 150 years ago – once again being placed at the very top of the civil engineer and politician's agenda.

The stretch of line washed away at Dawlish in Devon in 2014. (Colin J Marshal).

Chapter 6

Somerset and Bristol

■ Tunnelling ■ **Bath Abbey**
■ **St Mary's Church , Redcliffe**
■ The Severn Tunnel ■

Railway Notes

Tunnels have been a feature of railways since the earliest days. The nature of Britain's topography meant that an effective method had to be found to lay lines either across or around hill ranges like the Pennines, the Chilterns and the Cotswolds or the mountains of the Scottish Highlands, in order to ensure, whenever possible, level alignments and the least demanding gradients. Sometimes the most economical way of achieving a feasible route was by tunnelling rather than digging deep cuttings. In some places, for instance in heavily built up areas, short distance tunnels were the preferred option since they caused least disruption to the surrounding conurbations. However, to complicate matters further, several landowners, whose properties were to be crossed by the early railways, demanded that tracks be hidden from view and this could only be achieved by tunnelling or digging a cutting and then roofing it to create a false tunnel; this was known as the 'cut and cover' method of construction. Miners formerly employed in coal mines or with experience of digging canals were the early builders of railway tunnels. Today, highly sophisticated tunnel boring machines, using the latest technology and precision guidance systems, can achieve routes through rock to within centimetres of their target. The Channel Tunnel and the east to west Crossrail link under London are both examples of how the technology has been used in recent years. (See also Chapter 18).

The early tunnel builders faced many challenges. Flooding was always a hazard while the nature of the ground through which they had to work almost invariably caused a variety of difficulties. As time passed, tunnelling methods became more efficient and the ability to pump out water and to line the inside of tunnels, usually with bricks, both improved. The basic approach to construction was to make a number of exploratory borings from above to determine the nature of the strata and to then connect these by digging pilot headings from opposite directions, gradually creating an underground route. Surveying of routes and work methods improved but it was not until the mid-nineteenth century that steam engines were used for some surface activities, although the

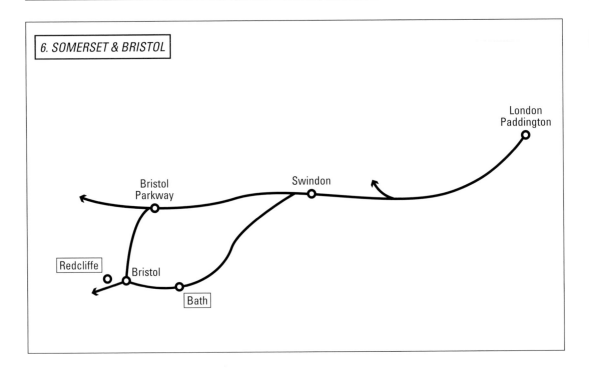

6. SOMERSET & BRISTOL

London
Paddington

Bristol
Parkway

Swindon

Redcliffe

Bristol

Bath

HSTs line up to leave Paddington Station.

miner, with explosives and a shovel and his faithful horse, remained for many years the principal means of cutting rock and removing it from the tunnel face. Working underground was always a hazardous occupation and inevitably lives were often lost. One hundred died between 1836 and 1841 alone during the construction of Box Tunnel near Bath.

As might be expected, it was the great railway engineers like father and son Stephenson, Locke and Brunel who led the work of building the early railway tunnels, nearly all of which remain in use today. One of the earliest constructions was a number of tunnels built under Liverpool to reach Lime Street station, completed in the late 1820s under the direction of George Stephenson. Others followed rapidly and the trans-Pennine tunnel at Standedge, operational in 1840, was for a long time the longest railway tunnel in Britain. However, it was eventually eclipsed by the building of a four mile tunnel beneath the river Severn to carry the main line from London to South Wales on a more direct route than that originally used via Gloucester. Both Box and Twerton tunnels, either side of Bath, were built by Brunel, and each has a castellated façade adding to the grandeur of their construction. It is said that the sun shines through Box tunnel at sunrise one day each year – April 9th – Brunel's birthday!

Another example of Victorian determination was the Woodhead tunnel, which carried the Sheffield to Manchester route under the Pennines in the Peak District. Built originally with two bores, it was later expanded to four parallel tunnels each three miles in length. Following rationalisation of the rail network in the mid-1960s the route was closed and the tunnels abandoned except for the installation of some high voltage electricity cabling. Considering the immense human effort expended on their original construction by teams of Victorian navvies, it is sad that today no role can be found for such an engineering achievement. A great debt was owed

Box Tunnel near Bath. (SSPL)

to the original builders and it is to be hoped that the tunnels might one day again see the passage of rail traffic.

The story of the Severn Tunnel is given later in this chapter. Meanwhile, some of the longest tunnels on Britain's transport network are those under London, built in the nineteenth century to enable people to move around the city more easily. Eleven sub-surface or deep underground routes connect from the centre to the suburbs, the longest continuous stretch being just over seventeen miles. The first line to be built was the Metropolitan in 1863 and of the overall 249 route miles in use today, forty-five per cent are underground.

Bath Abbey

A thousand year old place of worship which has in its time been a cathedral and an abbey and which today is a magnificent parish church. Important as the church where the first king of a partly united England was crowned.

Look for the west front with its 'ladders to Heaven'; the window in St Alphege's chapel showing King Edgar's Coronation in 973 and the fan vaulting above the nave and quire.

People have worshipped in Bath for over a thousand years. The city is probably as famous for its Roman buildings as anywhere in Britain but later conquests have equally left their mark on the city. The Romans left Bath in the fifth century to be replaced by Saxon invaders

The West Front with the façade showing a heavenly hierarchy.

The Edgar window in St Alphege's chapel.

who built a monastery there in 757. Three hundred years later around 1090, the Normans began a cathedral and this survived until the fifteenth century when the present abbey was started. All these churches stood on more or less the same site close to the river Avon.

The first king of England, Edgar, was crowned in Bath in 973. His coronation united the Saxon kingdoms of Wessex, Mercia and Northumbria and Bath, standing on the Avon, was on the boundary between the first two of these kingdoms. Dunstan, the Archbishop of Canterbury and Oswald, the Archbishop of York, both attended the ceremony which is recorded in a window in St Alphege's Chapel at the east end of the north quire aisle. A service attended by Elizabeth II in 1973 marked the thousandth anniversary of Edgar's crowning. Alphege was a later Abbot of Bath who became Archbishop of Canterbury in 1005 when, six years after his appointment and following capture, he suffered horribly at the hands of the Viking invaders for his refusal to order his people to pay the ransom demanded for his release. He was beaten to death 'with ox bones and the heads of cattle' according to the *Anglo Saxon Chronicle* and quoted in the guide book.

Bath and Wells were from an early time linked as religious centres and have remained joined under the diocesan jurisdiction of the Bishop of Bath and Wells ever since. Today, the Bishop's *cathedra* is at Wells but in 1090, Bishop John de Villula moved his throne to Bath where it remained until 1244 when it was transferred back to Wells. By all accounts during this period, the cathedral at Bath was probably twice the size of the existing church. However, by 1499 the Norman cathedral had fallen into a state of disrepair, whereupon began the construction of today's abbey church.

Standing before the west front of the Abbey presents an imposing sight. The Benedictine monks who began the rebuilding of the Norman cathedral at the end of the fifteenth century knew what they wanted to achieve when they created a façade emphasising what at the time was believed to be the place of God in the lives of the people, the position of the king above all others, the central role of the church hierarchy and the subservient position of the ordinary man. The exterior of the front shows Christ in Majesty at the apex with Henry VII below, above the main door. Ladders on either side, adorned with angels shown climbing up and down, led the way for the righteous to eventually access heaven and the afterlife. This was the message which the church wished to promote since it confirmed its central role in the lives of the people, although it was a theme which was soon to fade as the emerging message of Protestantism gave rise to a perception of a more personal relationship between God and the individual.

At the end of the fifteenth century, Bishop Oliver King led the work of rebuilding the former Norman cathedral. This reconstruction proceeded slowly and was only partly completed by the time of Henry VIII's reformation in the 1530s, a cataclysmic event which was to have consequences for the whole church and beyond. At that juncture the incomplete church became the local parish church, although it was not until 1616 that it was finally in full use.

The Abbey seen from the windows of an approaching train.

The ladders to heaven at the West Front.

The vaulted roof.

Inside, the west window is called a Pentateuch window, so described since it contains scenes from the first five books of the Old Testament. The window was completed in 1894 with panels showing the escape of the Israelites out of slavery in Egypt, celebrated every year at the time of the Passover. Below the window is the west entrance, solid oak doors embellished with heraldic shields given to the abbey in the seventeenth century in commemoration of the Montagu family, one of whom, James, had been the local bishop in the early years of that century.

The church is built of Bath stone which gives it a light appearance – causing the exterior to glow – while helping to brighten the many memorial tablets arranged around the walls. One on the north side of the nave commemorates Sir Isaac Pitman, a nineteenth century inventor who created the system of shorthand writing; the publishers Pitman were based in Bath for many years. Another tucked away in a corner of the north west entrance to the nave celebrates the Revd Thomas Malthus, who towards the end of the eighteenth century forewarned of the consequences of overpopulation and exploitation of the world's natural resources.

Much redevelopment work was carried out by Sir George Gilbert Scott in the 1860s, including replacing the 250 year old wooden roof of the nave with the striking stone vaulting which balances similar vaulting above the quire, dating from the sixteenth century. The now continuous vaulted ceiling must be one of Bath's most spectacular features. Gilbert Scott's radical work apparently completely changed the nature of the church's interior, showing it as it is today.

The east window dominates the sanctuary at that end of the church and shows fifty-six scenes from the life of Christ; it was damaged in the Baedecker bombing raids in 1942 and was restored by Michael Farrer Bell, the great grandson of the original creator. Four modern statues are placed either side of the window; from the left that of St Alphege, holding the bones used in his murder; St Dunstan, one of the archbishops who crowned Edgar in 973; Bishop Oliver King, whose vision led to the building of the present church; and John de Villula who moved the bishop's seat to Bath in 1090. These four statues reflect the most important historical events in the life of this great church, their respective stories telling us how the Abbey has developed and changed as generations have come and gone, each bringing their own interpretation of how it might be better prepared to face the future.

St Mary, Redcliffe

A most elegant inner city church in Bristol whose origins go back to the twelfth century and with maritime connections to the discovery of the Americas.

Look for the vaulted roof and its bosses, the Canynges memorials, the north porch and the model of the *Matthew* above the door.

St Mary's association with those seafarers who set sail from Bristol to discover America from the fifteenth century onwards is easy to understand. The early church had been built on high ground only a short distance from the wharfs and docks from where voyages began and sailors would attend the church before setting out and on return. God's blessing was considered important to the success of their endeavours and the church on the 'red cliffe' was the natural place to attend to seek his blessing or to give thanks for a safe return.

The proportions of the church suggest that those who built it and those who later re-modelled it may have seen it as a future cathedral. Its fine lines and the stone vaulted roof with its delicate ribs and bosses, of which there are over a thousand, all give an impression of a special place. Most of the roof work was accomplished by fifteenth century masons, although there are areas of the building, notably the inner north porch and St John's Chapel, which date from as early as 1185. Meanwhile, most of the glass is Victorian.

The Church from outside.

The Lady Chapel.

The spire built above the north porch rises to a height of 292 feet and is one of the tallest in England. It collapsed in the fifteenth century but was restored 400 years later. The fourteenth century porch is formed in the shape of a hexagon with inner and outer areas where, until the time of the Reformation, the niches were filled with statues of kings. It is considered one of the church's finest features.

Connections with Bristol's seafaring past are not hard to find. In 1497 John Cabot left to discover America, his voyage having been financed by the Sheriff of Bristol on the orders of Henry VII. Five hundred years later a re-enactment of that voyage of discovery took place using a replica of Cabot's ship, the *Matthew*. A model of the ship is now positioned above the inside door of the porch. Possibly the greatest benefactor of the church was William Canynges who in the fifteenth century owned nine ships and employed 800 sailors. He was variously the Member of Parliament and mayor of the city, the latter appointment being held for five terms. A monument in the south transept depicts Canynges and his wife while, to one side is a second monument of Canynges alone, in this instance shown as a priest, as he took holy orders following his wife's death.

Another connection with the Americas is a monument to Admiral William Penn high up at the west end of the church. Penn was a supporter of Oliver Cromwell in the Civil War and commanded his fleet; on the accession of Charles II, he placed the fleet at the king's disposal, an offer gratefully accepted, after which Penn led an expedition which captured Jamaica. He loaned much of the wealth obtained from this and other expeditions to the king who was in an

Looking east.

... years of
Pilgrimage
Prayer

Leaving Harbour & St Mary Redcliffe by Samuel Jackson c1825 Bristol Museum & Art Gallery

When ship-loads of medieval Christian pilgrims set off together 'To seek St James in Spain and St Peter in Rome' some of them left England from the busy port of Bristol. They had long and dangerous journeys ahead of them.

'September, return of the Pilgrims from Santiago de Compostela' Musee Conde, Chantilly, France / Bridgeman Art Library

Many would visit St Mary Redcliffe, towering above the city, to ask for a blessing before leaving. The Outer North Porch was begun about *1320* and inside was a shrine to St Mary the Virgin, mother of Jesus, patron saint of the church, sometimes known as Mary, Star of the Sea. A link with this ancient shrine has been made by commissioning an icon to replace it.

Imagine a pilgrim or a merchant preparing to cross the sea in a wooden ship, with only the stars and the sailor's skill to guide him. Perhaps he knelt to say the rosary, passing the smooth beads between his fingers as he recited the well-known words of his prayers. Months later, he might have returned to offer a prayer of thanks.

People still come here to offer up their prayers. Many will light candles, just as others have done before them, for nearly 900 years.
All are welcome to do so.

The candle is a symbol for Jesus, Light of the World, and represents a prayer being offered to God.

The Pilgrimage prayer.

impecunious state. On Penn's death, his son William called in the loan but accepted a grant of land in lieu on condition that it be named after his father; hence the naming of Pennsylvania.

The Handel window in the north ambulatory reflects a close relationship between the composer and Rev Thomas Broughton, Vicar of St Mary for a period in the eighteenth century. Handel lived in London during the time of the Hanoverian kings and apparently looked to a visit to Redcliffe to escape the Royal Court! Moving to the east end, the window in the Lady Chapel, badly damaged by bombing in World War Two, has been replaced by glass inserted in the 1960s. Designed by Harry Stammers of York, its vivid colours have managed to replicate the original dedication of the window.

St Mary, Redcliffe must vie with Bristol Cathedral for the accolade as to the finest church in Bristol. However, Elizabeth I was seemingly in little doubt as to the elegance of St Mary's when in 1574, on a visit to Bristol, she is said to have referred to it as 'the fairest, goodliest and most famous parish church in England'.

The church is surrounded by an area of green, formerly a burial ground, with some tombstones remaining. On Good Friday 1941, an air raid on the city resulted in considerable destruction around the church although it was not damaged. However, following a direct hit, a section of tramline was catapulted into the air and landed in the churchyard where it remains today, a symbol of how the church might nearly have been destroyed during the long years of the Second World War but nonetheless survived. Also in the churchyard is a stone commemorating 'The Church Cat 1912-27'.

Railway Notes

The tunnel linking the English and Welsh sides under the river Severn was opened in 1886. It took nine years to construct and at a length of 4 miles and 629 yards is the longest mainline railway tunnel in Britain. Two and a quarter miles are under the water and the deepest part of the river, known as the Shoots, is 45 feet above the rails. The greatest threat to successful completion of the project occurred when an underground spring, later named the Great Spring, burst into the tunnel in 1879. The workings were totally flooded and it took over a year for drainage to be effective in restoring working conditions. The problem of the spring, which brought fresh water from the Welsh side into the site rather than sea water from the Severn, was eventually solved by sealing it off and installing powerful pumps to ensure water levels should never rise beyond a certain level. Later, after the two pilot headings met in 1881, the Great Spring again broke through, while in October 1883 a further chapter of accidents led to flooding when one of the largest pumping engines broke down and water entered the tunnel from the English side, stranding eighty-three men who had to be rescued by boat. However there were no fatalities during the nine years of construction.

The tunnel is a fitting monument to the Victorian engineers who persevered to build it. Today it carries up to 200 trains a day while the pumps, originally steam driven by coal fired boilers but now powered by electricity, extract several million gallons of water every 24 hours to keep the tunnel dry. Strict operating procedures are in place to ensure the safety of those using the tunnel; for example it comprises a single signal section to ensure that only one train is permitted in the tunnel at any one time while clear rules govern the transit of trains transporting hazardous loads such as petroleum products. The route to South Wales will be electrified at some future time, a relatively straightforward task given the physical clearances allowed for by the Victorian engineers in their construction, but the erection of overhead line equipment and their maintenance in such a damp environment will take time and skill.

A GWR express between the wars.

West Midlands

Great Malvern Priory.

Chapter 7

Gloucestershire

■ What causes service disruption ■ **St John the Baptist Church, Cirencester**
■ **Tewkesbury Abbey** ■

Getting There

Cirencester does not lie on a railway line and is best reached via Kemble, six miles away, on the Swindon to Gloucester route; there are some through trains from London Paddington but most journeys will require a change at Swindon. Travelling time to Kemble is between an hour and a quarter and 90 minutes.

Further north Ashchurch, the station closest to Tewkesbury, is situated on the cross-country main line from Birmingham to Bristol but there are no through trains originating from London. Trains to Cheltenham or Worcester from Paddington, or to Birmingham from Euston, will, by either route and following a change, generally allow Tewkesbury to be reached in under three hours from the capital.

Railway Notes

As railway companies developed in the nineteenth century, they needed to create communities which could undertake the many functions required to sustain operational train services. Locomotive and rolling stock construction, research and design to aid future development, the training of railway staff and managing the timetable and infrastructure all required dedicated staffs if rail transport was to deliver the service advertised to the public. At the same time, companies had to remain competitive in the rail market. How and where these staffs came to be established is covered in Chapter 11.

Before the days of computers and electronic communications it was left to the human being, his ability to lead and manage groups of people and his knowledge and experience of how rail services should operate, to provide the skills to make the railway system work effectively. The railway companies of the late nineteenth and early twentieth centuries were part of a proud and highly disciplined service industry which in time came to realise that co-operation in providing co-ordinated services was probably preferable to the commercial rivalry engendered by a host of small companies operating in their own interests. This realisation, along with financial imperatives, led eventually to the creation of the 'Big Four' railway companies in 1923, following legislation by Parliament to provide the legal framework for a much reduced and more effective geographical grouping within the industry.

When everything is functioning well there is nothing as impressive as a railway system. However, contingencies can and do arise to disrupt the smooth running of trains, on occasions quickly degenerating into long delays and a perception of chaos to those unfamiliar with the system. The reasons for this are not hard to find and vary from unexpected events or unavoidable breakdowns to the occasional deliberate actions of those intent on causing disruption for their own ends.

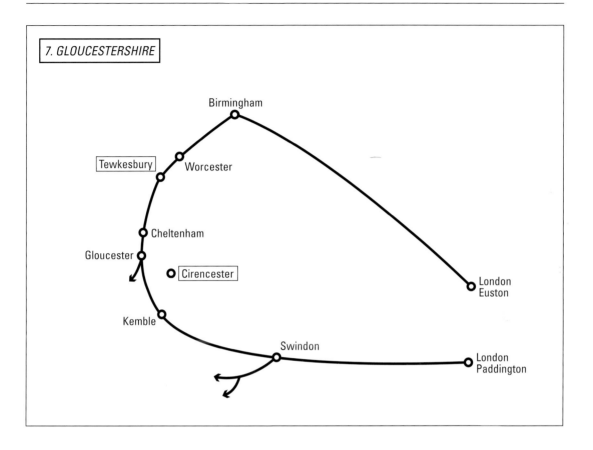

7. GLOUCESTERSHIRE

Birmingham

Tewkesbury | Worcester

Cheltenham

Gloucester

Cirencester

Kemble

Swindon

London Euston

London Paddington

To the passenger there must be fewer more annoying announcements than to hear that their train is to be delayed because of a 'signal failure' or that old chestnut 'leaves on the line'. Equipment can fail and track can be damaged, often following prolonged bad weather; both events usually the cause of late running or the cancellation of services. The immediate reaction of the traveller will be to assume that such conditions could have been avoided; however that may not be entirely fair. The truth lies between failures caused by poor management and, more often, failures arising from circumstances outside the control of those responsible. Railway infrastructure is intensively used and relies upon many miles of cabling and track which cannot always be closely inspected without the use of unsustainable levels of manpower and, by their very nature, railways are extremely vulnerable to outside interference. It is also true that our railway system has suffered lower levels of investment than required to permit the regular modernisation of services. Seventy years after the Second World War and only following privatisation in 1998, is real new investment now beginning to be seen and the precarious nature of the nation's finances can still threaten the delivery of long overdue programmes, as the announcement of delays to several electrification projects in the middle of 2015 made very clear. However, some of these schemes have since been reinstated in the forward programme.

An altogether more insidious threat lies in the occasional disruption of the network through industrial action. I have long wondered why the British railway network is more prone to stoppages from strikes than those of our Continental neighbours; after all the Swiss and the Germans, both of whom have systems that are highly efficient, seem by comparison to be almost strike free. In

A Network Rail train run during 'the leaf fall period' to ensure running rails maintain maximum adhesion for locomotive wheels by squirting a chemical onto the running lines.

Britain, relations between employer and employee can and do break down leading in the worst case to industrial action and travel disruption, sometimes so severe as to result in the national economy being damaged. The reasons underlying such actions are often hard for the travelling public to understand and strenuous efforts are today made to reconcile the parties involved; indeed strikes are fewer than they were but when they occur can cause considerable dislocation. No one would argue the necessity for unions and their role in safeguarding their employees' positions but the power they hold should be exercised with discretion and responsibility. Equally it behoves employers to behave realistically in the changes they may from time to time wish to promote .

Maybe we should take a leaf out of the book of those continental railways where management and union representatives meet in 'supervisory boards' to reconcile opposing views before industrial action occurs, the whole process being underwritten under the tenets of corporate law.

St John the Baptist, Cirencester

An imposing Cotswold church sustained by the wool trade in medieval times.

Look for the vaulted roof of the south porch, the hour glass pulpit, the height of the nave and the Boleyn Cup.

Long before Christianity firmly established itself in the area, Cirencester (Roman *Corinium*) had been developed as an important centre, where in Roman times three great, paved roads intersected, part of a network which connected the military outposts of their empire in Britain. One was the Fosse Way which ran almost straight from Bath to Lincoln by way of Cirencester. In the ninth century a Saxon minster was built in the town, which in its turn was superseded by an Augustinian abbey founded by Henry I three hundred years later. The abbey was built to the east of the Saxon minster, which was finally demolished when the present parish church was established on an adjoining site around 1150.

St John's is the largest parish church in Gloucestershire, larger even than some Anglican cathedrals. It took a long time to complete the building and extensive re-ordering of the structure took place between 1450 and 1530. Money from Cotswold wool would have financed the construction in the same way as local wool financed similar churches in Lincolnshire, the East Riding and elsewhere. It is easy to forget that in the fourteenth and fifteenth centuries, the development of the wool trade was probably an event of equal importance to the dawn of the industrial revolution four hundred years later, for the opportunities and riches that each bestowed upon those who grasped the chance to innovate and were prepared to take risks. Guilds or staples in which farmers and merchants combined to market their products were established and wool merchants became very wealthy, as did the ironmasters and coal owners of the 1800s.

The guilds may have financed much of the building of St John's, including the tower erected in 1400, and the nave. Conflicts between the abbot and the townspeople were a regular occurrence and disputes not uncommon until the time of the Dissolution. Thereafter, the church suffered

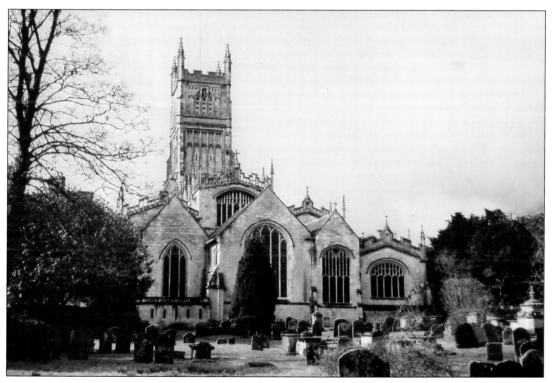

The Church.

The Boleyn Cup.

neglect, with glass being damaged and wall paintings obliterated by the random application of a lime wash. Between 1865-7, George Gilbert Scott undertook a major renovation which went a long way to restoring the building's fortunes.

The church is light and airy; the nave has soaring Perpendicular arcades with much clear glass in the side aisles. The south porch constitutes the main entrance with a fan vaulted vestibule, above which are a number of rooms, intended by the builders to be the place from where the business of the church and abbey could be supervised. The porch is Cirencester's most celebrated feature.

There are a number of chapels adjacent to the main body of the church, no doubt originally intended as chantries where prayers would be said or sung for the souls of the departed, in this case probably merchant families grown wealthy on the wool trade. The Lady Chapel was built in 1240 and extended 200 years later. The chancel is the oldest part of the church having been begun in the twelfth century, while the east window beyond is filled with glass from the fifteenth and sixteenth centuries; care of the glass was often neglected with the lead holding individual pieces in place being allowed to decay, while some windows were smashed at the time of the Civil War when the church was used as a temporary prison for captured Parliamentary troops.

Other features are the fourteenth century font – at one time used as a garden ornament in a house close to the church – and the 'hour glass' pulpit from approximately 1450. The latter gets its name from a directive by the bishop in 1630 that sermons should not exceed one hour, some preachers having apparently previously declaimed for far longer; the hour glass can still be seen to one side of the pulpit. Another unusual feature is the Boleyn Cup – located in an alcove by the entrance to the chancel – made in 1535 and engraved with the badge of Anne Boleyn, the second wife of Henry VIII, who was executed in 1536. It was presented to the church by Dr Master, physician to Anne's daughter, Elizabeth I. On the nave piers are a number of carved and coloured shields of local people who have over time contributed to the wellbeing of the church.

St John's, one of England's finest 'wool churches', is full of history and, as might be expected, closely reflects the fortunes of the town and its citizens over several centuries. Today it stands next to the market place, hemmed in by houses and shops, but as important as ever as a local centre of worship in the Cotswolds. John Betjeman in Collins *Guide to English Parish Churches* describes it as, 'The largest and most splendid of the Cotswold wool churches, it is also perhaps the most beautiful in all England.'

Tewkesbury Abbey

A glorious church which has seen much history and conflict in its 900 years.

Look for the Norman nave, the arches of the west end, the Milton organ and learn about the great families who have nurtured the abbey over hundreds of years.

It would be hard to select any one of the magnificent medieval churches or cathedrals lying along the line of the river Severn south of Worcester as being the finest, but Tewkesbury Abbey would surely rank high amongst the contenders. The abbey stands on a flood plain where the Severn is joined by its smaller tributary the river Avon, flowing from the north-east. This confluence of two major waterways can make the church quickly vulnerable to the threat of flooding in periods of heavy rainfall, a contingency often foreshadowed in the past, but its position provides an incomparable setting for the abbey church.

As in so many other places in Britain, a rudimentary church may have been built at Tewkesbury during Saxon times. However it was not until the Norman era that a more substantial building was begun in 1087, when Robert Fitzhamon, a loyal supporter of William II, was given land by the king and established an abbey there, the monks being brought from Cranborne in Dorset. The abbey was finally consecrated in 1121. Further developments proceeded over the next three hundred years with the building of a stone vaulted roof, the rebuilding of the quire and some

The Abbey.

The West End.

eastern areas of the church, the construction of chantry chapels for some noble families and the rebuilding of areas damaged by fire.

The Norman character of the church is very pronounced. The west front comprises six rounded arches with a fourteenth century window within. The nave with its sturdy arches, the transepts, quire and most of the presbytery are all Norman, while the east end, the attendant chapels and the ambulatory, are mainly fourteenth century as is the intricate vaulting of the roof. The tower is of massive proportions, being one of the largest and best examples of its construction anywhere in the world. There are fourteen arches carrying the nave roof, each more than thirty feet high and over six feet in diameter. Because the original roof was replaced in stone and later lowered the original clerestory arcade was reduced in extent.

A stone *pulpitum* or screen originally divided the nave from the quire but this was later removed and replaced by a wooden screen making it possible to look along the length of the church. Much of the original detail has been lost, including the painting of some of the interior. Moving east, much alteration took place during the first half of the fourteenth century when the quire arches, originally as high as those in the nave, were reduced in height, while five chapels were built at the east end around the early apse. In the twelfth century, Abbot Alan was sent to Tewkesbury from Canterbury where he had previously been prior; on his death in 1202, he was buried in a tomb which was later transferred to one of the chapels. Having been at Canterbury at the time of Archbishop Thomas Becket's murder in 1170, he was allegedly able to recount the circumstances of the saint's martyrdom.

It is probably the events leading up to the Wars of the Roses for which Tewkesbury Abbey is best remembered. For centuries prior to the fifteenth century, a series of noble families ruled the area, working with – or against – reigning monarchs depending upon alliances struck or feuds engineered to ensure their position and prosperity. After the death of Robert Fitzhamon in 1183, his daughter Amice de Clare completed the abbey tower, her family subsequently being closely involved in events culminating in the sealing of Magna Carta in 1215. Linked through marriage, the de Clares and later the Despenser family continued their support for the abbey, in 1320 beginning to rebuild parts of it.

However, the fourteenth century was the prelude to more violent times in the following century, the Despenser line passing to the Neville family, one of whom, Richard Neville, was later ennobled as Earl of Warwick, a pivotal figure in the Wars of the Roses. He first espoused the Lancastrian cause and supported Henry VI, before later switching his allegiance to Edward IV and the House of York. Known as 'the Kingmaker', Richard of Warwick continually intrigued to gain his own ends but was finally defeated by Edward at the Battle of Barnet in April 1471 and killed. Three weeks later, a second battle took place at Tewkesbury, the Lancastrians again being defeated with Edward, Prince of Wales, son of Henry VI, being killed and later buried under the Abbey tower. During the battle Edward IV and his troops entered the abbey church in pursuit of the fleeing Lancastrians but were confronted by the abbot and forced to withdraw, although eventually capturing their enemy. Fourteen years later, the Wars of the Roses eventually ended

The nave looking east.

Choir practice before Evensong.

Tom Denny's modern window in the chapel of St. John the Baptist.

when Henry Tudor defeated Richard III and the Yorkist army at Bosworth Field in Leicestershire in 1485.

In 1540, the abbey at Tewkesbury was dissolved and the abbey sold to the local people. The purchase enabled the church to be protected to a great extent, although many of the monastery buildings were demolished

Much of Tewkesbury's stained glass is medieval, including that in the quire windows and at the west end, while in other areas the glass is Victorian. The abbey guide explains the windows and the noble families commemorated in the quire glass, some of whom have already been mentioned in this chapter. In 1987, to mark the 900th anniversary of the founding of the abbey, Tom Denny created two windows in the Chapel of St Catherine and St John the Baptist: he took as his theme the Benedictine adage 'to work is to pray'.

The Milton Organ, now in the church, is so named because it is said once to have been played by the great poet John Milton, Latin secretary to Oliver Cromwell in the mid-1650s. Originally built by Thomas Dallam, a well-known Jacobean organ builder who intended it for Magdalen College, Oxford, it later found its way to Hampton Court Palace (where Milton is said to have played it) before being returned to the college. In 1737 it was moved again, this time to Tewkesbury where it has resided ever since. It is said to be a particularly fine example of its time and is greatly treasured at the abbey.

Time spent at Tewkesbury must be time well spent under any circumstances but on the late summer afternoon when I visited, the abbey positively shone. Its 900 years of history are so important and interesting that it must be a stop on the itinerary of anyone interested in England's great churches.

Chapter 8

Worcestershire

■ Bridges and Viaducts ■ **Pershore Abbey** ■ **Great Malvern Priory**
■ The Severn Valley Railway ■

Getting There

Both Pershore and Malvern can be reached from London Paddington using the Cotswold line to Worcester and Hereford. Journey times are two hours to Pershore and two and a half hours to Great Malvern.

Railway Notes

Bridges, large or small, are an essential part of any transport route, be it rail or road. By constructing bridges and viaducts the early civil engineers used their skills to ensure the routes they built were as level as possible and crossed waterways or valleys on as straight and level alignments as was feasible. Tunnels (see Chapter 6) were often constructed for similar reasons, it usually being economically preferable and often easier to go through or over an obstacle rather than to build a diversion to avoid it.

Today's travelling public probably gives little thought to the many structures their train may pass over or under during the course of a journey. There may be literally hundreds of them and only the largest or most renowned like the Forth Rail Bridge in Scotland or the Royal Albert Bridge linking Devon and Cornwall, will catch the attention of the passenger as a train crosses. However, without them, journeys would be far longer in time and distance and more expensive.

Viaducts differ from bridges in that they are usually longer and are characterised by the generally narrower size of individual arches and the greater height of the piers. The construction of brick built structures began in the 1830s when railway engineers erected bridges as part of the early routes. The Royal Border Bridge at Berwick on Tweed enabled the East Coast line to Scotland to be completed in 1850, while the Ribblehead viaduct on the Settle to Carlisle railway was finished twenty-five years later; its twenty-eight arches, each at a height of 104 feet, stand as a permanent memorial to those who built that wonderfully engineered line across the Pennines.

Over the last two hundred years, cast iron, steel and reinforced concrete, as well as brick, are all materials used to build bridges and viaducts. The Menai Straits, the stretch

Trackwork.

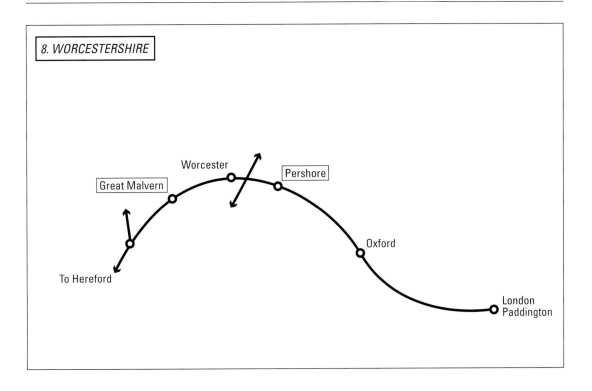

of water separating the Isle of Angelsey from the Welsh mainland, demonstrates the innovative approach taken by engineers in the early nineteenth century when deciding how best to cross an obstacle. The straits are a fast flowing stretch of water, dangerous under most conditions and hazardous to cross by ferry. Thomas Telford chose a suspension road bridge design for the first crossing which was completed in 1826. His plan relied upon massive stone arches and piers on either bank between which were strung a number of huge chains which, when raised to the required height, carried a roadway strung from vertical chains. The bridge has been modified and reconstructed several times since.

It was first envisaged that trains would cross the road bridge to reach the island with individual carriages being uncoupled and then drawn across by horses. However it was soon realised that such a process would be far too slow and cumbersome and in the late 1840s Robert Stephenson, George's son, decided to build a dedicated railway bridge. He chose a tubular bridge design, utilising two immense iron tubes or boxes which rested on three limestone piers; the railway tracks were to be enclosed within the tubes. Construction was far from easy but the bridge was opened in early 1850 and carried a double track railway to the port of Holyhead.

The Britannia railway bridge is 'guarded' by four lions at the two ends; they were carved by John Thomas who did similar work at the Houses of Parliament and at Buckingham Palace. However, in 1970 a disastrous fire inside the tubes, started by youths hunting bats, caused the bridge to sustain severe damage, to the extent that the structure had to be comprehensively rebuilt, the opportunity being taken to support the bridge decking on additional arches and to convert the bridge into a double deck structure; a single track railway below and a roadway above. Thus today, the rail bridge is but a shadow of its former self. Meanwhile, plans to build a third crossing over the straits have been under discussion since the end of the last century.

Reproduction of Terence Cuneo's painting of the Britannia railway bridge across the Menai Straits, prior to the fire of 1970. (SSPL)

The longest viaduct in Britain.

The longest viaduct in Britain is the Harringworth viaduct, which crosses the valley of the river Welland close to the boundary between the counties of Northampton and Rutland. Completed in 1878, the structure is 1,275 yards in length and comprises eighty-two arches, each with a forty foot span. It is the longest masonry viaduct across a valley in Britain and a Grade 2 listed structure. Closed to all but freight traffic in the 1960s, it is now transited each day by a single passenger train between St Pancras and Melton Mowbray, although the line is also used by diverted passenger trains and freight traffic.

Arguably the most graceful of large railway bridges is that built by Brunel to carry the Great Western railway across the river Thames at Maidenhead. It is formed of two 128 foot semi-elliptical spans. Completed in 1838, critics said it would never succeed but Brunel knew better. It was the subject of a famous watercolour painted in 1844 by J M W Turner; *Rain Steam and Speed – The Great Western Railway*. I wonder today how many passengers being conveyed west from Paddington Station ever give a thought to Brunel's marvellous structure as their train crosses it in a matter of seconds?

Pershore Abbey

An abbey reduced to a broken church in 1540 but since restored.

Look for the vaulted ceiling, the Crusader's tomb, the lantern tower and the Norman font.

The early history of the abbey at Pershore is not easy to follow. 681 is said to be the date when an endowment for a religious community was made by Ethelred, King of Mercia, followed eight years later by the establishment of a monastery. The story of that monastic settlement is incomplete, but there were apparently periods of relative peace when the kingdom of Mercia was ruled by a succession of strong monarchs, interspersed in the ninth century by more violent times when Viking raids and periods of Danish rule led to frequent disruption. In 972, St Oswald, Bishop of Worcester, decreed the use of the Benedictine Rule by the monks and thereafter life may have settled down, although there were further difficulties soon afterwards when moves were made to restrict the expansion of monastic lands, depriving a large part of the settlement.

A Norman abbey was built between 1090 and 1130, although a series of serious fires resulted in the building having to be remodelled on several occasions. The oldest parts of the church remaining today are the south transept and the north side of the tower, both of which are Norman, while the original apse and the sanctuary at the east end and the present nave – formerly the Monks' Quire where the monks would have participated in services at all hours of the day and night – date from the Early English period.

When the abbey was dissolved in 1540, the abbot handed it over to Henry VIII, the monks being dispersed into the local communities to become priests, with the Monks' Quire then becoming Pershore's parish church, purchased for four hundred pounds. A letter, allegedly written by a monk at the time to Thomas Cromwell, Henry VIII's chief minister, records a plea for the monastery not to be touched, clearly to no avail.

In common with some other monastic churches recorded in this book, on dissolution Pershore Abbey church was considerably reduced in size, the original nave being truncated where it

The abbey.

The ploughshare lierne vault above the quire.

joined the western side of the tower. Further deterioration occurred in the seventeenth century, when the north transept collapsed as a result of which over time a number of buttresses have been put in place to hold the western part of the church in position.

The tower of the abbey, built upon Norman piers in the early fourteenth century, is often compared with that of Salisbury Cathedral for the magnificence of its design and construction. Restoration by Sir George Gilbert Scott took place in the 1860s including the opening up of the tower lantern and the exposure of the internal panelling while further work was undertaken again in 1936 when the north transept became the vestry. As a result today's church is a mixture of styles which the guide book does its best to unravel for the visitor. The former quire vault with its 'ploughshare' lierne design and bosses is probably the highlight of the church; there is one boss on the north side dubbed the 'laughing boss' which shows an amused face surrounded by foliage. The bosses were originally painted, as indeed was the interior of the church itself, and many have grotesque faces similar to the green men which appear in many English churches.

The south transept contains a tomb, originally in the churchyard, of a Crusader knight and is thought to date from the late thirteenth century. It is a fine example of its kind, in particular its armour which is described in detail by the guide book. On the north side of the west door is the Norman font, restored to the abbey in 1921 having been once used as a cattle water trough before residing in a private garden. All the stained glass in the church dates from the latter half of the nineteenth century.

There is a clutch of mainly Norman churches in South Worcestershire and neighbouring Gloucestershire: the cathedrals at Gloucester and Worcester; the abbeys at Pershore and Tewkesbury and Great Malvern Priory, all within a few miles. Undoubtedly they drew upon each other, exchanging ideas, copying practices and trying to decide how best to react to the policies and later the demands made by Henry VIII and his advisers when the greatest upheaval in the life of the nation took place in the sixteenth century and continued for nearly a century thereafter. If there is a particular strand running through this book it is how politics – royal and church – and growing pressure for reform of the Roman Catholic Church during Tudor times, led to the demise of the great religious houses which had exerted such an influence over the lives of people for so long. Pershore was amongst the most prominent of these churches to be dissolved.

Great Malvern Priory

A wonderfully sited church, light and bright inside, with much of historical interest.

Look for the fourteenth century glass, the Norman columns in the nave with their mason's marks, the Magnificat window and the medieval tiles at the east end.

Nestling in a fold of the Malvern Hills, surrounded by the houses of Great Malvern, the priory presents a most pleasing prospect, especially on a warm and sunny summer morning. Inside the building, the church presents an equally delightful spectacle, light and airy with no screen between nave and chancel to restrict the overall impression; the church was a haven of tranquillity in the hour or two I explored its interior.

A local monk built the first priory in 1085. Aldwin wished to found a monastic settlement in the Malvern area but initially found the task overwhelming and almost abandoned the project. Wulstan, Bishop of Worcester, implored him to continue and, with a charter from William I secured, Aldwin persevered and completed a Norman priory, a smaller version of today's church. A feature of the building is the surviving robust Norman pillars and the arches of the nave. If you look at the walls of today's nave you will see a clear difference in the materials used; below are pieces of the rough locally quarried stone used by Aldwin and his helpers, while higher up are more neatly cut sandstones used when the priory was redeveloped in the middle of the fifteenth century.

Redevelopment, begun in 1440 and taking sixty years, forms the basis of the church today. All the glass was installed during this period, although Henry VIII's Reformation meant that the Benedictine monks had little time to enjoy the completed spectacle. The Bishop of Worcester, Hugh Latimer, petitioned Thomas Cromwell to exclude the priory but without success and the monastery was dissolved, the church being saved by the payment of twenty pounds from the local

The priory.

townspeople. Bishop Latimer was one of three Protestants later burned at the stake on the orders of Queen Mary during the brief period in the middle years of the sixteenth century when Roman Catholicism was re-established. The other two martyrs were Archbishop Cranmer and Nicholas Ridley, a former Bishop of Rochester.

The priory escaped without appreciable damage in the Civil War but the eighteenth century saw a period of severe decline when little was done to effect serious repairs, until 1860 when a large sum of money was raised allowing George Gilbert Scott to implement a programme resulting in the preservation of today's fine church. Meanwhile, only three of the monastery's original buildings survived the Reformation of which only one remains today, the gatehouse, now the Malvern Museum.

The glass in the west window was donated in the 1480s by Richard of Gloucester, later Richard III. The window was later blown out in a gale and the original glass was placed in other windows in the church. The replacement glass now in the window is also medieval, showing an array of bishops, saints and angels; included are St Christopher carrying a child on his shoulders, St George slaying a dragon and St Laurence holding a gridiron. Below the window are six tiny apertures sited in pairs; known as squints, they may originally have been intended to allow those unable to attend services for reasons of age or infirmity, to do so from a passageway behind the west window. Chapter 13 records a squint in Selby Abbey established in that church for similar reasons.

The nave and the west window showing the squints.

A mason's mark on a pillar in the nave.

Already mentioned is the magnificence of the nave with its sturdy Norman columns. The second pillar from the lectern on the north side shows several clearly visible masons' marks, scratched on the surface to record who was responsible for its construction. It was a common practice to mark a workman's labour in this way – often to ensure later payment for the work done – and there are plenty of examples elsewhere in other churches; at Malvern the letter S was probably used to identify an individual craftsman although when the church was painted, the mark would have presumably been obliterated.

The north transept houses the Magnificat window given to the church by Henry VII in 1501. It records the words of that canticle in which Mary praises God for making her the mother of Christ. Mary is shown in the upper part of the window, circled in blue, accompanied by some of the patriarchs, but some of the other depictions including that of God and Christ, have been lost. Lower down are pictured Henry VII and his eldest son, Prince Arthur, who died aged sixteen and is buried in Worcester Cathedral.

As you move east into the chancel, look for the misericords in the quire stalls, wonderfully expressive depictions of the seasons and other scenes from everyday life; one records a doctor's visit while another shows a woman berating her husband and making him pull off her boots! The east window is claimed to be the largest such window in a parish church in England and depicts the Passion, Crucifixion and Resurrection. In the north quire aisle are two millennium windows

A misericord showing a man pulling off his wife's boots.

The north side of the Priory.

constructed by Tom Denny in 2004 to mark the beginning of the third Christian millennium, while St Anne's Chapel on the south side contains some well-preserved fifteenth century windows recording many facets of the Old Testament. At the east end are a series of medieval tiles showing a wide variety of subjects ranging from biblical events to animals, badges of the nobility and scenes of everyday life. These were made locally in a kiln close to the church – discovered in 1830 – and were produced in large numbers, some subsequently finding their way to Westminster Abbey and St David's Cathedral in West Wales.

There is so much to see at Great Malvern and the current guide book excels for its information and interest. I could have spent more time there and would recommend a visit to anyone; indeed it is a place I hope to visit again.

Railway Notes

The Severn Valley heritage railway runs for sixteen miles between Kidderminster in Worcestershire and Bridgnorth in Shropshire. It was originally part of a network of lines managed by the Great Western Railway which radiated from Birmingham to serve destinations in the West Midlands. The line was never strategically very important although it did provide a second route from the Midlands to Shrewsbury, a link which proved useful in the Second World War. It followed the river Severn for much of its course through glorious countryside. Built by the Great Western

Two views of the SVR at Bewdley.

Railway between 1858 and 1862 the line was never a financial success and was closed in its entirety as a public service in 1963.

The section of the line running north from Kidderminster to Bridgnorth was reopened in 1970 when the Severn Valley Railway, now a heritage line, started operating from Kidderminster where the route connects with Network Rail tracks. Today, a comprehensive service is run generally using steam locomotives and rolling stock of the steam era. For those interested in how railways first operated and were then developed during the eighteenth and nineteenth centuries a visit to the SVR is a must. Its stations, signals and trains exude the atmosphere of the Great Western Railway.

What is the future for such lines? Lovingly cared for by volunteers with specialist staff present to supply the expertise necessary to ensure safe operation, heritage lines like the SVR, the sixth largest in the country, fulfil an important role as a tourist attraction and provide an opportunity for those whose interests lie in the study of railways. In addition, each railway makes a contribution to the economy of the areas through which it passes, an important consideration when pondering the way in which the leisure market has grown in recent years.

There are over one hundred heritage lines across Britain; they are professionally run and provide a useful if not a vital service. In time they may grow in importance as the means by which we choose to move around this crowded island changes in the face of climate change and allied pressures. I spent a morning at Bewdley on a fine summer's day in August 2015 watching the way the SVR operated. The day took me back to what life on the railways in the inter-war years must have been like; steam traction, unhurried train movements, courteous staff, mechanical signalling, passengers' luggage piled on the platforms beside stacked milk churns and absolute peace once a train had departed until the arrival of the next. Everybody present seemed pleased to be part of a scene representing a bygone age when Britain changed the face of the world in inventing and promoting steam railways.

SVR between Kidderminster and Bridgnorth. (Lewis Maddox)

Chapter 9

Shropshire

■ Railway signalling and the Quintinshill disaster
■ St Laurence, Ludlow ■ St Mary and St Chad, Shrewsbury ■

Getting There

Ludlow lies on the line connecting Shrewsbury and Newport (South Wales). The town has no direct service from London and passengers will need to travel there changing at one of the above two places. This will mean an overall journey of between three and four hours from the capital. Direct trains to Shrewsbury from Euston take approximately two and a half hours, while those to Newport from Paddington two hours. Ludlow is under an hour from Shrewsbury and about ninety minutes from Newport.

Railway Notes

Planning and executing the safe passage of trains has been the foremost duty of managers, engineers and staff from the earliest days of rail transport. From the middle years of the nineteenth century when for the first time trains ran under their own power along a dedicated track, human beings have had responsibility for ensuring their safe passage. At some stage flagmen, drivers, signallers, station staffs and controllers have all had a role in ensuring that a train moved safely from one place to another with passengers never being put at risk. Technical innovation and the development of control systems and, more recently, the use of computers has meant that safety has increased progressively as manually operated mechanical equipment has, in many instances, now come to be replaced by digital based control systems. However, an individual driver or signaller is still ultimately responsible for the safe running of a train.

These short notes cannot discuss all aspects of railway signalling and will concentrate primarily on what travellers may observe on a journey. Three basic elements comprise a signalling system: Line side structures to indicate to a driver the state of the line ahead and the route to be taken at a junction: interlocking devices which prevent a signaller setting up a route which could conflict with another route already cleared for a train, which, if permitted, would result in a collision; finally a system of sectional 'blocks' or signalled sections needs to be established to ensure a safe distance between trains travelling in the same direction, thereby eliminating the possibility of a collision from the rear. These three basic principles and the practices and regulations underpinning them are enshrined in the 'rule book', the bible for all railwaymen involved in the operation of trains.

Flagmen walking in front of a locomotive ensured the safe movement of the first trains. They were subsequently replaced by highly visible line-side structures, mostly semaphore signals painted to be easily recognisable. These signals evolved to fulfil two basic purposes. A red 'home' signal which if at danger required a train to stop and a yellow or 'distant' signal with a 'fish tail' at one end, which gave warning that a driver should slow down in anticipation that the next signal would be at danger and he must therefore be prepared to stop. The earliest semaphore signals,

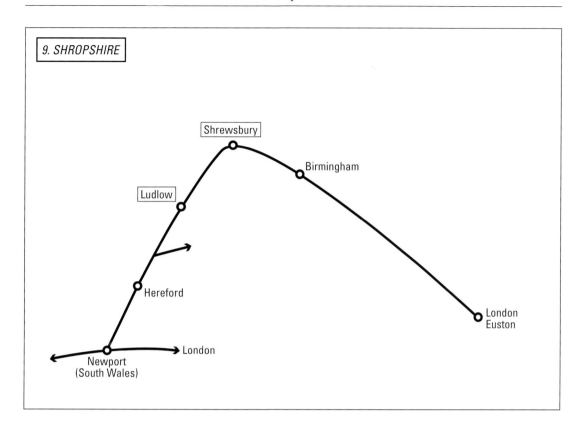

Ludlow on the Marches line. A local train arriving from Shrewsbury.

The LNWR Signal box at Shrewsbury built 100 years ago.

Interior of a country signal box – Severn Valley Railway.

termed 'lower quadrants', indicated danger or caution when the signal arm was in a horizontal position, but that it was safe to proceed when the arm was lowered at an angle of forty five degrees. Later lower quadrants were generally replaced by 'upper quadrants' which indicated the line ahead to be clear when the arm was raised at an angle of approximately forty five degrees. This change of positioning ensured that if a signal malfunctioned - for example, if the wire from the controlling signal box was severed - the arm would automatically come to rest in the horizontal or danger position. While upper quadrant signals tend to proliferate in most areas of the country, lower quadrant signals are still to be found in large numbers mainly on the territory originally covered by the Great Western Railway.

In the twentieth century, colour light signals started to replace semaphores on many routes, showing a red, yellow or green light. Their meaning was quite clear and the development of this type of signal allowed several aspects to be shown in a single signal; for instance under the block system a single yellow would indicate only one section ahead to be clear, two yellows two sections and a green three or four. With sections being anything up to a mile or longer in length this told a driver how he should proceed, allowing him to calculate his speed in the knowledge that he might be liable to be checked at some point further along his route. Such a system has successfully managed train movements for decades and, despite the parallel use of in-cab signalling based upon a system of 'ship to shore' telephone links between a signaller and a driver permitting direct speech, line side signals, semaphores or lights, will still be needed for some time to come.

Automatic Train Control systems which warn a driver of the aspect shown by an approaching signal have been in use for many years. A more detailed description of the early Great Western Railway automatic train control system is given in Chapter 4 of *England's Cathedrals by Train*. Such systems are today widely deployed, both in Britain and across Europe and are being improved all the time, amongst other advantages now permitting the locomotives of one nation to run on the railways of another, a development which should eventually lead to a more seamless pattern of train travel across Europe.

An interesting derivative of upper quadrant signals is their use in the Pass of Brander in Argyll to warn of possible rock falls. Here, the single line railway to Oban passes between Ben Cruachan and Loch Awe with little space on either side. In order to warn drivers of boulders falling onto the track, trip wires are laid parallel to the line for over six miles connected to seventeen semaphore signals. Should a rock fall occur the trip wire would be severed, automatically causing the signals, normally indicating a clear aspect, to return to indicate danger. This ingenious method of protecting against an unpredictable danger was first introduced by the Callander and Oban Railway in 1882. However, in 2010 it did not prevent a train striking a small boulder and being derailed.

The successful and safe operation of a railway depends ultimately upon strict discipline. As already said, the rule book caters for all eventualities and, if followed, should minimise the risk of accidents. Sadly this was not the case at Quintinshill north of Carlisle on 23 May 1915 when the worst accident in British railway history occurred. A troop train travelling from Central Scotland to Liverpool and carrying soldiers of a territorial battalion of the Royal Scots destined to embark for Gallipoli, ran into a local train standing on the wrong line, after which the wreckage was smashed into by an express to Glasgow running northwards at speed. Fire then broke out. 226 people, mainly soldiers, died with almost another 250 injured. The accident was caused to a large extent by a failure to observe the rules for handling train movements.

Meanwhile, the systems used to communicate the signaller's instructions in order to control a train's movement have been modified and improved over time. Around a century ago there

Stone signals above Loch Awe.

Stone signals.

were probably 2,000 working signal boxes on Britain's railways, each controlling short sections of line and the trains using them. By the 1960s this had been reduced to about 800. The trend today is towards 'signalling' longer stretches of track from signal centres, placing control of routes increasingly under one centre. These signalling centres could in time have responsibility for covering vast distances, including controlling level crossings, although the intention is to eventually replace as many as possible of these by bridges. However, signal boxes still exist and come in all sizes; the interior of the box at Bewdley is shown with this chapter while one of the largest operational signal boxes left on Britain's railways is still in use at Shrewsbury, a massive structure built over a hundred years ago by the London and North Western Railway.

An array of upper quadrant signals at the National Railway Museum.

St Laurence's Church, Ludlow

A fine fifteenth century church close to the Marches and Wales.

Look for the hexagonal south porch, the windows in St John's Chapel given by the Palmers' Guild, the Jesse window in the Lady Chapel and Queen Elizabeth I's exhortation that parishioners should read the Ten Commandments.

Ludlow lies in the valley of the river Teme, an ancient town much fought over in medieval times and now an important local centre not far from the border between England and Wales. Its grand fifteenth century church has sometimes been described as the 'Cathedral of the Marches', signifying its ancient role providing a Christian presence in a place from where the Lord President of the Marches ruled Wales and the neighbouring border lands on behalf of the monarch. The term 'marches' may have been first used in the Domesday Day book of 1086 when William the Conqueror appointed three trusted nobles to garrison strategic locations along the border between England and Wales to control movement and resist attacks from the Welsh. The area covered ran from Chester in the north, south to Monmouth but was not precisely defined. Those appointed to secure the area were given certain privileges and had a degree of independence from the monarch. The roles of the 'marcher earls' as they came to be known were phased out in the sixteenth century.

The town also has an equally imposing castle, the centre from where the Council of the Marches controlled Wales under the rule of Tudor and Stuart kings. Ludlow saw particular savagery in the closing years of the Wars of the Roses as the fortunes of rulers and their opponents ebbed and flowed. The church guidebook states that the present church has 'evolved over more than 800 years'. Going back in history, it is held that there has probably been a place of worship in Ludlow since pre-Christian times, later followed by a Norman church, itself rebuilt at the end of the twelfth century, from which today's church was then developed in the fifteenth century.

One of the earliest Tudor visitors to Ludlow was Prince Arthur, eldest son of Henry VII who married Catherine of Aragon in 1501 but died shortly afterwards of sweating sickness, a common precursor of death in Tudor times. Arthur had been created Lord President of the Marches two years earlier by his father and installed in Ludlow Castle. Following his funeral at Ludlow, Arthur's body was buried at Worcester Cathedral. Catherine was later betrothed to Arthur's brother, Henry, who in time succeeded to the English throne as Henry VIII with all the consequences which were to follow for Church and State and Catherine herself

Most of the church is in the Perpendicular style and in its early years was cared for by the local Pilgrims' or Palmers' Trust. A palm denoted pilgrimage – and then only to the Holy Land – and until the Reformation priests selected by the trust conducted worship and ministered to the Palmer congregation. The south entrance to the church is a hexagonal porch similar to that at St Mary, Redcliffe in Bristol – see Chapter 6 – and opens out into the nave where the moulded columns rise to the roof giving a distinct impression of openness and space. Originally the nave would have been bordered by chantry chapels and murals but these were removed at the time of the Reformation. The result is a bright and welcoming building.

The massive fifteenth century tower is positioned at the crossing, with beyond it the chancel which is flanked by two chapels, St John's and the Lady Chapel. At 135 feet, the tower dominates the town and provides a beacon for the traveller journeying across the beautiful Shropshire

St Laurence's Church.

The west window containing images of nobles and others associated with Ludlow over the ages.

countryside. Originally, there was a rood screen dividing the chancel from the nave but this was later removed making the inside view from west to east even more spectacular. Work to develop the chancel began around 1433 and the quire stalls, misericords and the decorated ceiling are all worthy of study. Many of the misericords reflect human situations; a housewife at work in her kitchen while a barmaid, accused of giving short measure, is seen being taken off to Hell. Much of the chancel was restored in the nineteenth century.

Some of the glass in the church is medieval although much was restored in the nineteenth century. The Lady Chapel has a fine Jesse window in which Jesse can be clearly seen lying at the foot. A window on the south side of the chancel at the eastern end contains parts of a former window which originally depicted the Ten Commandments; today's reconstruction warns against theft, adultery and the sin of coveting one's neighbour's house. Although mainly later reconstructions, the windows at the east and west ends of the church – both bright and cheerful – and those in St John's Chapel where the original glass was given by the Palmers' Guild in the fifteenth century, and in the side aisles, are all of interest.

There is a tiny plaque in the Lady Chapel recording that in 1669 the local fire tenders were housed there; it is interesting to discover how many churches were used for this purpose three or four hundred years ago. Another feature of Ludlow, drawn to the visitor's attention in the guidebook, is a board in the church which records Elizabeth I's exhortation, given in parliament,

The Tower.

that the Ten Commandments should be displayed in churches. The board at Ludlow was erected in 1561, surrounded with symbolic Tudor roses, but is unique in that the wording of the last commandment 'Thou shalt not desire thy neighbour's house' is apparently only to be found in Ludlow.

One of Shropshire's best known citizens was the scholar and poet, A E Housman. Famous for his series of poems, *A Shropshire Lad*, he died in 1936 and his ashes were buried in the St Laurence churchyard. Meanwhile, a quilt celebrating the poem's centenary was made in 1996 and is in the church.

St Mary's Church and St Chad's Church, Shrewsbury

Two churches in the heart of the town now linked in a single parish.

Look for the medieval glass and Dutch roundels at St Mary's and the Puritan Balcony at the back of the church. At St Chad's enjoy one of the few round churches in England and find some interesting memorials.

The ancient town of Shrewsbury, the county town of Shropshire, stands almost surrounded by a meandering loop of the river Severn; 'within the river' are four churches while others, including the Abbey, lie outside. My researches suggested to me that descriptions of two of the churches within the old part of the town might be of greatest interest to a visitor. I therefore decided to include them rather than the Abbey. St Mary's in the east is covered first followed by St Chad's, built on a bluff above the Severn about half a mile to the west of St Mary's.

Closely surrounded by houses, the church of **St Mary** comes upon the visitor rather suddenly although from further afield the tower at 222 feet high is easily discernible above the roof tops. An original church is said to have been built around 960 by Eric the Peacemaker, but nothing of substance remains and in the middle of the twelfth century it was replaced by the present Norman building. That church has since been redeveloped in some areas in the Gothic style, with medieval glass said by Simon Jenkins in his *England's Thousand Best Churches* to be of a comparable standard to that found at Ludlow and Great Malvern. The east window comprises an almost complete Tree of Jesse, installed in 1792, which was originally in an earlier St

Railway poster depicting the delights of Shrewsbury.

St Mary's showing some the Flemish glass.

Chad's Church and was transferred from there when the tower collapsed in 1788. The interior of St Mary's is rather dark, sandstone being the material, with a panelled roof decorated with bosses and carvings of angels.

Some of the windows in the side aisles are filled with Flemish glass of the fifteenth and sixteenth centuries, much of it collected by a vicar of St Mary's in the first years of the eighteenth century. Clearly he travelled widely on the Continent discovering examples of Belgian, German and Dutch glass and returning with them to Shrewsbury. Some pieces tell the story of a saint, in one case the life of St Bernard, while the Dutch roundels contain biblical and apocryphal stories. They provide an interesting study and would appear to be quite exceptional. Amongst the oldest property in the church are the *sedilia* close to the altar which date from around 1150.

At the back of the church high up on the south side is the Puritan Balcony. It was from there that, according to the church guide pamphlet, Francis Talents, the rector during the period of Oliver Cromwell's Commonwealth, chose to address an assembly of worshippers 'since he preferred to barrack, curse and preach to his congregation from behind so that they will focus on their prayers and God'. Meanwhile, the church porch contains two tenth century tombstones, the only remnants of the original Saxon church.

At the other end of the main street linking the two churches is **St Chad's**, a total contrast with St Mary's and one of the few round churches in England. The original St Chad's, located nearer the centre of the town, was thirteenth century but was virtually destroyed when the tower collapsed, an event compelling the move to the present site. Perched on a hilltop overlooking the river, the Georgian church, designed by George Steuart – also the architect of nearby Attingham House – was built in 1790 and has a Doric portico which gives access to the body of the church, described by Simon Jenkins as 'a wide galleried amphitheatre supported on Ionic and Corinthian columns', the entrance being in the style of a country house. Such is the difference between this church and so many others described in this book that it was most refreshing to enter such a place, especially as the smell of the flowers was so overpowering!

The three stage tower above the portico changes from a square to a circle with a dome resting on top. The box pews are arranged in a concentric layout facing east to a large window above the

A country train with a typical cross section of passengers.

St Chad's Church.

The interior of St Chad's showing the Ruben's triptych copy.

The interior of St Chad's.

sanctuary, a depiction of Ruben's triptych in Antwerp Cathedral. The window, which is in three sections, was presented to the church in 1842 by the Rev Richard Scott and is fully explained. The carved reredos below is a war memorial dating from 1923.

There are many memorials in the church and its adjoining chapels, many containing plaques commemorating soldiers fallen in war, including from local regiments such as the King's Shropshire Light Infantry and the Herefordshire Regiment, both now subsumed into larger regimental units. However, they are still of enormous importance to those families who have for centuries lived in the Marches, from where on innumerable occasions their ancestors would have mobilised to defend the nation.

One particular memorial to catch my eye was a tablet recording the life and achievements of John Simpson, who died in 1815. He was the builder of St Chad's, a distinguished engineer who also constructed the bridges over the Severn at Bewdley and across the river Tay at Dunkeld, the canal aqueducts at Poncysylte and Chirk and the locks and basins on the Caledonian Canal; a fine example of Georgian enterprise and skill so typical of the pioneers of the Industrial Revolution.

St Chad was originally raised at the Lindisfarne monastery on Holy Island. He became Bishop of Lichfield in 669, a man greatly loved for his humility and saintly disposition. The church in Shrewsbury which carries his dedication, is today joined with St Mary's in a single parish. St Mary's is now in the care of the Church Conservation Trust.

North West

The view of Cartmel Priory showing the tower set at an angle of 45 degrees to the building.

Chapter 10

Cumbria

Getting There

Communities in West Cumbria are connected by a railway line which leaves the West Coast Main Line at Carnforth and, after travelling north for almost 100 miles, reconnects into the same route at Carlisle. It serves the coastal towns of Barrow in Furness, Workington, Whitehaven and Maryport by a meandering route on its long odyssey from north to south. Train services are essentially provided for local travel and are neither fast nor necessarily comfortable, most rolling stock now being overdue for renewal. For those wishing to travel beyond the county's boundaries, a change is required at Lancaster in the south or Carlisle in the north, although some trains now link Barrow directly to Manchester Airport. Trains from London Euston take under three hours to reach Lancaster, from where a local train should be used to Grange-Over-Sands, the nearest station to Cartmel Priory and a journey of approximately 25 minutes. The priory is approximately three miles from the station.

Reaching Lanercost Priory requires a journey of just under four hours from Euston to Carlisle. From there a train to Brampton on the Newcastle route or a bus could be used; however the remote location of the priory suggests a taxi may be the best option.

Railway Notes

A feature of the Cumbrian coast line is its regular use for the carriage of hazardous nuclear materials. Special armoured flask wagons hauled by pairs of diesel locomotives are used to move radioactive fuel rods or waste materials to and from the power station and processing plant at Sellafield to similar locations in Britain. Corresponding movements take place between other nuclear power stations located around the coast and transport by rail is generally acknowledged to be the most secure and efficient way to move such materials. Strict operating standards are rigorously applied and accident prevention measures regularly practised, involving all the agencies likely to be called upon in an emergency. There has been no major incident involving these nuclear trains in the time they have been running on a regular basis. Other substances of a dangerous or hazardous nature are also handled by the rail freight companies, including petroleum products, chemicals and aviation spirit, although increasingly, fuel can now also be moved long distances through a network of underground pipelines.

On the southern section of the coastal line lies the village of Ravenglass, which lends its name to the Ravenglass and Eskdale Railway, a narrow gauge line built in 1873 to transport hematite iron ore from mines in the hills near Boot to the coast, from where it was then taken by standard gauge railway to Barrow. The line was laid to a gauge of 3 feet between the rails and in addition to transporting iron ore, it also carried passengers. Forced to close in 1913 following the collapse of

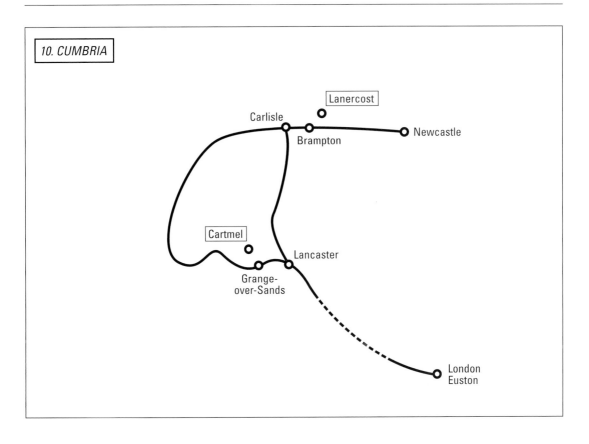

Ravenglass and Eskdale Railway. (Peter Mills, Ravenglass and Eskdale Railway)

the economic case for its continuation, the line was only saved in 1915 when two model locomotive builders decided that it could provide an ideal venue to trial their engines. The line was re-laid but this time to a gauge of one foot and three inches. Thrown that lifeline, the route again saw the carriage of quarried stone in the 1920s, something which continued until 1953.

Today, the line continues to carry passengers the seven or so miles up Eskdale. In 1959, the Ravenglass and Eskdale Railway Preservation Society was formed, leading to the refurbishment of much of the line and the modernisation of locomotives and rolling stock. It provides a favourite tourist route for those wishing to penetrate the Lake District National Park to learn something of the lives of the people who lived and worked there 150 years ago. It is the one of the oldest and longest narrow gauge railways in Britain, affectionately known as La'al Ratty or 'little railway' in the Cumbrian dialect.

Cartmel Priory

A spectacular Norman priory which celebrated the 800th anniversary of its foundation in 1988. The bell tower with the belfry placed diagonally to the base is unique in England.

Look for the different styles of architecture and in particular the Norman arches in the chancel. Find the twenty-six misericords in the quire stalls and the remaining panels of the Jesse window in the Town Choir.

It is claimed that Cartmel was first mentioned in historical records in the late seventh century, when land there was granted to St Cuthbert by Egfrith, the King of Northumbria. The area was wild and barren, exposed to attack by raiders from the sea, lying as it does on a peninsula between the mouths of the rivers Kent and the Leven, each of which flows into the dangerous waters of Morecambe Bay to the south. How the local community developed is not recorded and it was not until the end of the twelfth century that a religious settlement was founded on the site.

William Marshal, later created Earl of Pembroke, came from humble origins. At the age of five he was taken hostage by King Stephen against the good behaviour of his father, who had become involved in the arguments surrounding the legitimacy of Stephen's right to succeed Henry I on the latter's death in 1135. However, young Marshal quickly learnt the skills and practices required to make his way at the Royal Court. Thereafter, he served in the household of Henry II and travelled to the Holy Land as a surrogate crusader for the king's son, also named Henry, who had died in 1183. On his return, Marshal was readmitted to the royal household and granted land at Cartmel, where in 1189 he founded the first priory buildings. So indispensable did Marshal become to the monarchy that Richard I permitted him to marry into the nobility. Later created an earl, he acquired great wealth and became involved in the bargaining which preceded the sealing of Magna Carta in King John's reign. He was appointed Regent of England when John died in 1216 and for a time had care of his son, Henry III.

The priory guide states that it is unwise 'to speculate why a person chooses to follow a particular course of action' but goes on to suggest that 'it is reasonable to assume that gratitude to God for his good fortune was at least one reason why William Marshal founded a monastery at Cartmel.' The first canons came from Bradenstoke Priory in Wiltshire, where Marshal's father was buried; they belonged to the Order of St Augustine.

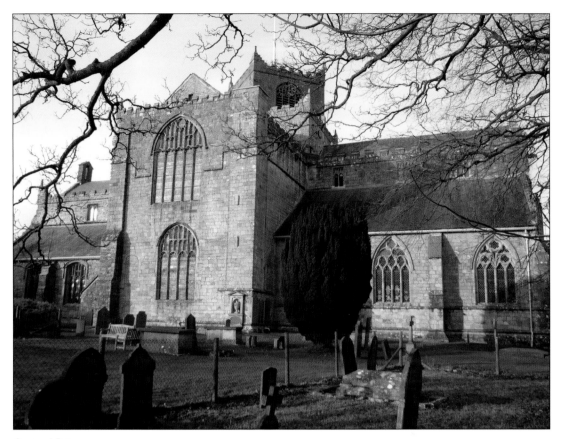

Cartmel Priory.

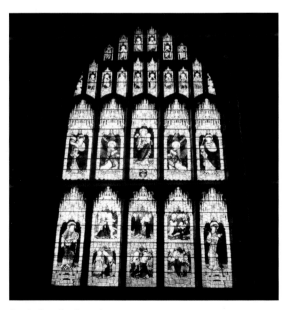

A window in the priory.

From the twelfth century, Cartmel Priory started to take shape. By 1250, much of the early church was complete except for an east window, the extended nave and the later stages of the tower. Carboniferous sandstone from a nearby quarry was used and since it occurs in distinct layers, each with different properties, the most appropriate stone was selected by the masons for particular areas of the building. At this stage, the church would have consisted of a chancel with its Transitional Norman arches, side chapels, a small lantern tower and a truncated nave. A variety of other buildings surrounded the monastery, including, no doubt, a chapter house, infirmary and accommodation. Following the instructions of William Marshal, local people have always been allowed to worship within the priory.

Disruption occurred in the early years of the fourteenth century, most notably when Scots raiding parties under Robert the Bruce damaged many of the outlying Priory buildings, although leaving the church more or less intact. Notwithstanding, work continued during the early part of the century with the Town Quire, on the south side of the chancel, being enlarged to accommodate a chantry tomb for Lord and Lady Harrington. The Jesse window was also placed in the east wall. Following this work, further development took place in the early 1500s with the building of a bell tower, the extension of the nave, the carving of misericord seats for the monks in the quire and the installation of the east window. When extended, the newly created belfry at the top of the tower was positioned at a forty-five degree angle to the original base, a feature believed to be unique in England.

By 1537, Henry VIII's commissioners had begun to implement his orders for the reformation of the monasteries, surveys having been conducted earlier to determine the action to be taken in respect of each settlement involved. Cartmel was no exception and it was decided that the monks should be expelled and the Priory's supporting buildings stripped of their valuable lead and destroyed. However, local people protested that the Priory church should be exempted since it was their place of worship where the altar had been gifted to them originally by William Marshal. Their request was eventually granted but not before rioting had broken out and four monks and ten laymen had been convicted of treason and executed at Lancaster Assizes. Their crime was to 'will, wish or desire treason' to the king.

Since the seventeenth century, the fortunes of the church have fluctuated. The chancel was re-roofed around 1620 but, twenty-five years later, Roundhead troops of Oliver Cromwell camped in the building doing considerable damage, including the destruction of the recently installed organ. The early eighteenth century then saw a long period of neglect and it was not until 1827, when a new vicar, Rev Thomas Remington, was appointed, that a comprehensive programme of restoration was begun and the church was given back much of its old style and elegance.

Located in what for many years must have been a remote and infrequently visited part of Britain, Cartmel seems to have escaped many of the events and disturbances visited upon other communities in the North of England. However, there was one local occurrence

A present day exhortation to remember William Marshal.

which regularly brought unwelcome news to the Priory community; before the building of the railway and a bridge across the river Kent, those wishing to reach Cartmel from the east had invariably to negotiate a route across the perilous quick sands and tidal waters of Morecambe Bay. Coaches and horses were used but many who attempted the crossing were caught by the tide and drowned. While some of the victims are buried in the churchyard, there is only one memorial in the church; it commemorates a man aged twenty-four who drowned on the sands where at the same spot and a year later, his mother also perished.

Today, Cartmel Priory is an important church, well visited and regularly used for worship by local people. Its place in history is well told in the church while Simon Jenkins in his book *England's Thousand Best Churches* describes Cartmel 'as the most beautiful church in the North West'.

Lanercost Priory

Another remote and peaceful priory church with the intact nave still used for worship, set in glorious Border countryside.

Look from inside at the view of the ruined areas of the original church, seen through the east window, the remnants of the Lanercost Cross in the north aisle and the statue of St Mary Magdalene below the apex on the outside wall of the west front.

There are several similarities between the priories at Cartmel and Lanercost: both were founded in the twelfth century; both began as Augustinian orders and both suffered attack by the Scots during the wars which raged between England and Scotland during the thirteenth and fourteenth centuries. Indeed, both priories probably attracted the personal attention of Robert the Bruce during his raids across the border.

Today, Lanercost is a wonderfully peaceful spot at which to stop and contemplate the modern world. Situated in the valley of the river Irthing, surrounded by lush woodland and pastures and only a few yards from a section of Hadrian's Wall, what remains of the original church offers a glimpse of history. Today, the church is still a place of worship, the responsibility of the Diocese of Carlisle, while the remaining buildings belonging to the priory are managed by English Heritage. There is a visitor centre nearby.

The Vaux family may have conceived the original idea of building the church, probably as a house of prayer or as a place where their remains might be buried. Building started around 1166 and an Augustinian foundation was possibly chosen because two neighbouring religious communities at Carlisle and Hexham had already embraced the Order. It is thought that in the twelfth century there were as many as 165 Augustinians foundations in the North.

The stone to build some parts of the priory church and its surrounding buildings is said to have come from Hadrian's Wall. A Lanercost Cross was carved to celebrate completion of the first phase of the church in 1214; it was originally placed outside the church but in the seventeenth century it was apparently broken and a section was used to cover a child's grave. Later, it was dug up and used in the construction of a barn until in 1888 it was moved into the church to its present position in an alcove in the north west corner of the original nave. An inscription on the stone recorded King John as being on the English throne and David I as ruling Scotland at the time of its creation.

The half ruined priory viewed from the north side.

The land either side of Hadrian's Wall was for centuries in dispute between the English and Scottish monarchs and Lanercost was often the objective of attack by raiders from the north. In 1280, Edward I first visited the priory, returning to the area again in 1306 when he stayed there for six months until the following Easter in order to conduct a campaign intended to bring Scotland under English control. For much of this time he based himself at Lanercost, his Great Seal being brought from London, indicating that where the king resided was where government of the realm would be discharged. This placed great pressure upon the priory, which was ill equipped to handle the administrative needs of the king and a large retinue of advisers and followers. Edward's last visit was in 1307 and, already in ill-health, he died shortly after leaving the priory.

Thereafter, the priory continued to be the subject of sporadic Scottish attacks for some years, with David II plundering the Treasury and pillaging the site in 1346. In a very real sense, the fortunes of the priory varied as relations between opposing monarchs fluctuated.

In 1532, in company with other monasteries, the priory was dissolved by Henry VIII's commissioners and the church fell into decline. The story of the Reformation is already well known and at Lanercost, once the lead on the outlying buildings of the priory had been stripped from the roofs, it was left to the Dacre family to take charge of the church on behalf of local people. Thus it remained, with worship being mainly confined to the north aisle of the nave.

The west front showing the statue of St Mary Magdalene given by Edward I in the fourteenth century.

Naworth Castle, a stone's throw from Lanercost, has been in the ownership of the Earls of Carlisle since early in the seventeenth century. Today it is the seat of the present Earl while another branch of the Howard family live at Castle Howard in North Yorkshire. In 1718, when the Dacre family line died out, the Howards of Naworth assumed responsibility for the priory and thereafter the nave was re-roofed and worship resumed there. Later in 1847 more repairs became necessary and further restoration was undertaken. In 1929, the priory ruins were bequeathed to the nation.

The interior of the surviving areas of the church, the nave and the north aisle, are used for worship. At the east end is a lancet window, through which can be seen the ruins of the original tower and transepts, a stark reminder of the size and magnificence of the original church. Above the nave are the arches of the clerestory, beautifully proportioned and with plain glass in the windows. There is no south nave aisle to match that on the north side, that being where the original cloisters would have been before the Dissolution. Outside high above the west front and its lancet windows, is a statue of St Mary Magdalene, to whom the church is dedicated, given by Edward I in the fourteenth century and positioned in an alcove.

The ruins are well maintained and official information suggests that, if ever wished, re-roofing of the derelict chancel might not be too difficult. Meantime, the priory church and its surroundings

Looking through the east window into the original priory ruins.

Remnants of the Lanercost Cross.

provide a wonderful place to contemplate history. Whilst reaching Lanercost by train may not be straightforward, a visit to this remote and formerly wild area of Border country must be a high priority for anyone interested in discovering how religion first established itself in the furthest corners of these islands and later weathered so many storms. Meanwhile a quotation from the Collins *Guide to English Parish Churches*, edited by John Betjeman, recording an impression of the priory at Lanercost seems to encapsulate the magic of the place:

'To watch through [the east] window sun and shadow dramatizing the soaring ruins of the transepts, tower and roofless choir outside, the walls still rising to their full height and carrying high up on one of them a Roman altar to Jupiter, one of the few in an English church, is to know life and death in the same moment.'

North East

Hexham Abbey.

Chapter 11

Northumberland and Durham

▪ The birth of railways on Tyneside ▪ **Hexham Abbey**
▪ The creation of the Tyne and Wear Metro ▪ **St Paul's Church, Jarrow** ▪

Getting There

Newcastle is a two hour and a half hour journey from London King's Cross. From there Hexham to the west is a thirty minute ride on a Carlisle train while, to the east, Bede, the station for Jarrow, can be reached in less than twenty minutes from Newcastle Central, using the Tyne and Wear Metro. It is a mile on foot to St Paul's Church.

Railway Notes

Tyneside could claim to be the place where railways were invented although other parts of the country may make similar claims, particularly Cornwall. From the eighteenth century onwards railways have developed, first as wagon ways with wooden rails, then as railways

A Tyne Valley local service at Hexham.

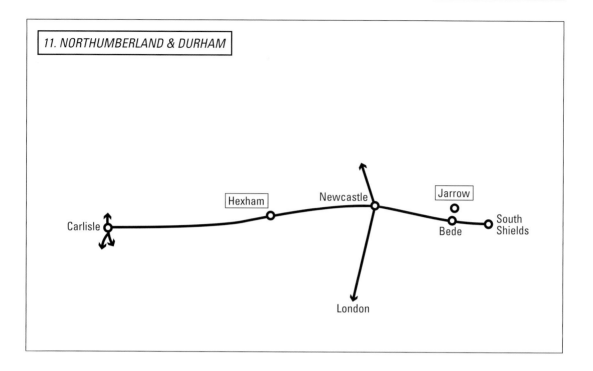

11. NORTHUMBERLAND & DURHAM

constructed to service coal mines using iron rails with wagons pulled by horses, until finally there developed steam locomotion and the present system of rail transport that remains such an important feature of our lives. These and other developments which led to the creation of railways – including descriptions of the lives of those most prominent in pioneering the changes which occurred –.are well documented elsewhere. This chapter looks only at the lives of two Tyneside engineers, George and Robert Stephenson.

George Stephenson is generally credited with developing the early locomotive *Puffing Billy* designed in 1813 by John Blenkinsop and William Hedley. Stephenson was born at Wylam to the west of Newcastle in 1781 and his early employment was as an engine-wright at a local colliery. Following his success with *Puffing Billy* he designed a locomotive which would eventually run on rails and haul carriages. *Locomotion*, built by his son Robert, was the result and ran at the opening of the Stockton and Darlington Railway in September 1825. That line, originally authorised by Parliament in 1821, was the first public railway to be built, although the Liverpool and Manchester Railway, opened in 1829, was the first to regularly haul passengers.

The Stephensons – father and son – were involved in nearly all these evolutionary developments, either in designing and building engines, creating railway routes or working to persuade a sceptical public that steam haulage was the technology of the future. George Stephenson was appointed as engineer to both the Stockton and Darlington and Liverpool and Manchester Railways and in October 1829 the *Rocket*, designed jointly by George and Robert, won the Rainhill trials held to identify the most suitable locomotive for the latter line. Thereafter, George went on to create other lines, to develop ever more efficient locomotives and to become a persuasive public advocate of this new system of travel. The name Stephenson is part of railway lore and stands alongside those other Victorian pioneers who led the nineteenth century Industrial Revolution. One of George's other inventions was a miner's safety lamp; it came to compete with the well known

Davy lamp and was allegedly used principally by miners working in the North East, being known as the Geordie lamp. This may be the explanation as to why people living on the north bank of the Tyne are today still called 'Geordies', although there are probably other equally valid explanations as to how the nickname first came to be used.

Hexham Abbey

One of the oldest foundations in the North of England with links to Roman and Saxon times.

Look for the Night Stair, the Frith stool, the panels and carvings on the Leschman chantry chapel and the Saxon crypt.

Hexham is a market town about twenty miles west of Newcastle just downstream of the spot where the northern and southern tributaries of the Tyne join to form the main river. It was at one stage the capital of the former county of Hexham-shire. In 674, St Wilfrid was granted land by Queen Etheldreda, the Northumbrian queen, to found a Benedictine monastery at Hexham, completed four years later.

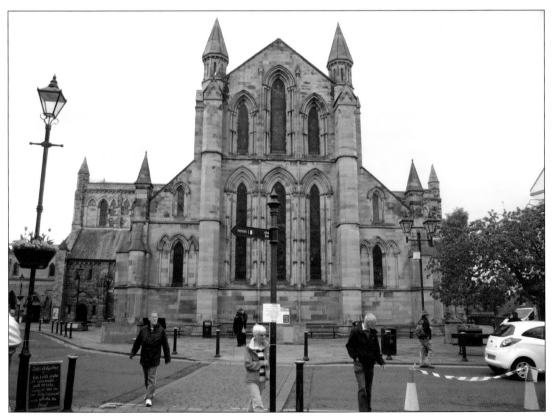

The East end.

The Frith stool in the quire.

Judging by where he travelled, the offices he held and the people he encountered and influenced, Wilfrid must have been one of the Church's most inspiring early bishops. Born in 634, he went to Lindisfarne to learn to be a monk after which he set out on a journey to Rome. Having travelled across Europe he returned to England and later became Abbot of Ripon where he built a church in 673. He also attended the Synod of Whitby in 664, when he persuaded the King of Northumbria to follow the church practices of Rome rather than those of the Irish Christians. He went on to become Bishop of York, although he was deprived of his position in 677. He was reinstated in 703, to his two foundations at Hexham and Ripon.

Queen Etheldreda was Wilfrid's benefactor. She was locked into an unhappy marriage with Prince Ecgfrith of Northumbria, from which she was desperate to escape in order to devote herself to God. Wilfrid intervened on her behalf and arranged a divorce in 670 following which, two years later, Etheldreda founded an abbey at Ely. (See Chapter 19 of *England's Cathedrals by Train*). Meanwhile, the grant of Etheldreda's dowry lands to Wilfrid helped with the building of his monastery in Hexham.

Wilfrid's church was burnt by the Vikings and re-founded in 1113 as an Augustinian priory by Archbishop Thomas of York. The only part of Wilfrid's church to have survived is the crypt which is now reached from steps in the nave. In the late thirteenth century, Tynedale and the surrounding area of Northumbria was raided by Scottish marauders and much damage was inflicted by William Wallace and his followers. The next two hundred years saw more peaceful times and improvements to the church, including the building in the sixteenth century of a

The 'Night Stair' in the South Transept.

wooden screen. In 1537, Henry VIII formally dissolved the priory.

The interior of today's church is quite dark. You enter through the Slype, originally the route by which the monks would have arrived into the building from the cloisters to the south. The south transept itself was completed in 1230. Reaching up from ground level along the west wall of the transept is a flight of steps connecting to the gallery above. This is a medieval 'night stair' which was used by generations of monks to walk from their dormitories, in order to attend nocturnal services in the abbey without having to leave the building. At the foot of the stairs is a Roman tombstone thought to have been dedicated to Flavinius, a soldier of the first century and possibly a standard bearer. It may have come from the Roman military cemetery at Corbridge, a few miles east of Hexham.

At the west end of the quire is the Frith stool, a Saxon *cathedra* or seat to be occupied by a bishop, which could possibly have been made for St Wilfrid. There is a similar seat by the high altar in Beverley Minster, described in Chapter 12. Either side of the quire are two chantry chapels, containing the remains of their founders and intended as places where masses could be sung to assist the passage of the departed soul on its journey to heaven. That on the north side is dedicated to Rowland Leschman, prior in the 1480s. The lower stone wall is carved with an array of images, some satirical figures, while more traditional figures of bishops of Hexham and a Dance of Death scene, a medieval depiction like the *danse macabre*, designed to explain the inevitability of death, are painted above. The chapel on the south side is dedicated to Robert Ogle, whose family had been locally important for many years; he died in 1409.

To the right of the high altar are the *sedilia*; carved in oak, they date from the early fifteenth century. The quire stalls are also probably from the same period and underneath are 'tip up' misericords which are to be found in many churches. Most of the glass in the abbey is eighteenth century or later, periods when areas of the church, including the nave, suffered decline but were restored through the efforts of active vicars and the rich donors whom they persuaded to underwrite the necessary work. An interesting reference in the abbey guidebook describes links to the Company of Mercers, the premier livery company of the 'Big Twelve in the City of London', which in 1625 gave a bequest 'to establish Puritan lectureships' in Hexham and other churches. The custom was discontinued from 1902.

There are many examples of Roman and Saxon carved stonework in the church which can be found by reference to the guidebook, while the display in the 'Big Story' Exhibition in the former cloister area adjacent to the west end, charts the history of the church and how it evolved over nearly twelve hundred years since St Wilfrid's time.

Railway Notes

Generally speaking public transport in Britain's biggest cities has been only slowly developed, in marked contrast to continental conurbations where the need for efficient, co-ordinated networks has always been better understood. London, Liverpool and Glasgow all had underground rail systems well before the Second World War but they were 'stand-alone' ventures, not necessarily integrated with other public transport provision. However, in 1980, Tyne and Wear, at the time one of Britain's metropolitan counties, began the construction of a metro system which was eventually to take over the management and running of local suburban rail, bus and river Tyne ferry services. As a result, the first fully integrated urban transport network in the country was formed.

With hindsight, it would seem manifest that the formation of such systems was common sense and indeed the building of not dissimilar networks in other cities like Sheffield, Manchester and Nottingham have all taken place since, but in 1984 the completion of the Tyne and Wear Metro or NEXUS was seen as revolutionary since it brought together transport agencies which, given past experience and left to their own devices, would have been unlikely to integrate.

The breakthrough on Tyneside was the decision to convert the existing British Rail 'heavy rail' suburban lines into a rapid transit system while at the same time extending lines into the heart of Newcastle, thereby giving better access and improving co-ordination with other agencies. In parallel, bus services were also restructured, with the public being encouraged to use 'park and ride' facilities to minimise the number of cars entering a city centre. At more or less the same time, the Government passed legislation to deregulate bus services, abolished the metropolitan counties, confirmed the local infrastructure to run the new services and, following the financial crisis of 1976, gave parliamentary authority for the necessary civil engineering work to proceed.

The metro was planned over a number of years and became operational in stages. The first lines began to run in the early 1980s, with the line to Newcastle Airport added in 1991 and that to Sunderland a year or so later. Today, routes are operated by efficient electric trains over a total

A Tyne & Wear Metro service at Bede station.

Maintaining the infrastructure. A Network Rail track recording train at Newcastle.

Rocket and George Stevenson's statue at the National Railway Museum, York.

of nearly seventy-five route miles. Six hundred staff are employed with an estimated 38 million passengers being carried each year.

From a railway perspective the line is interesting, since on certain sections 'heavy rail' trains operated by passenger or freight companies, occupy parallel tracks to those used by the Metro, thereby making the best use of existing structures like tunnels, bridges and stations. Meanwhile, 'light rail' vehicles or trams are cheaper to run and can operate on both railway lines and on tram tracks laid on streets conferring even greater flexibility. As a result, rail based systems have come to be recognised as the optimum way of providing for the mass transit of people and are now firmly established in nearly all parts of the world.

What might the Stephensons have made of such developments? No doubt they would be delighted that the railway revolution, begun by them and others in the early nineteenth century, was still progressing nearly two centuries later and that the first truly integrated urban light rail system in Britain should have originated on Tyneside.

St Paul's Church, Jarrow

One of the best known churches in Christendom with close links to St Bede.

Look for the oldest part of the church at the east end, the tiny glass windows in the south wall, the original dedication stone above the chancel arch and what is believed to be St Bede's chair.

The church at Jarrow must be amongst the most acclaimed of Christian shrines. Its antiquity and its historical connection to the Venerable Bede distinguish it as one of the most important sites in Christendom. Sadly its location in an area of dense urbanisation, only a stone's throw from the river Tyne a few miles upstream from South Shields, surrounded by industrial sites and shipyards, must inevitably diminish its aura.

However, the woods and well-tended lawns in the immediate vicinity of the church present a more attractive local picture. Approaching down a path through trees, you enter a church the interior of which is presented in a manner which immediately tells you that the place is lovingly looked after, indicating that at least some of those living nearby appreciate its importance and are determined to preserve it for future generations. To visit on a blustery day in May when showers and bright sunshine alternated, was stimulating.

The history of the church is straightforward. Completed in 681 on land given by King Ecgfrith of Northumbria, Bishop Biscop intended that Jarrow would complement the nearby monastery at Monkwearmouth, constructed only seven years earlier. His intention was that the monks from each should work together. After the original church – today's chancel – was completed, probably using dressed stone from nearby Roman buildings, a bigger second church was added at the west end – the site of today's nave – along with some other monastic buildings. This second church was later demolished and the present nave and north aisle were built in Victorian times by Sir George Gilbert Scott. Other changes have been made more recently.

As with most medieval churches, the fortunes of the Jarrow church fluctuated. The Vikings raided in 794 but the monastery was re-founded a hundred years later by Aldwyn, the Prior of Winchcombe in Gloucestershire and later became a subsidiary of the Benedictines at Durham.

The church from the south.

Looking east towards the original chancel.

The window in the Church thought to be the oldest stained glass in Europe, originally in the monks' refectory.

A replica in the church of the original dedication stone dated 685.

The outside ruins of the old church.

At the Reformation, it ceased to be a monastic settlement and became a parish church. Today it is looked after by the Jarrow team ministry.

Bede was born in the area and is thought to have entered the monastery at Jarrow about 685; apparently he recorded that there were 600 monks in the affiliated monasteries at Jarrow and Monkwearmouth in 716. Bede was both a very devout man and a person of great learning, in his time writing books of biblical commentary and detailing the lives of the saints. His greatest work was his *History of the English Church and People* which spread his reputation as an early thinker and writer far and wide. Bede died in 735 and his remains lie in the Galilee Chapel at the west end of Durham Cathedral.

The chancel at St Paul's is rich in history. The Dedication Stone of the original church is positioned above the Chancel arch; the inscription on it records that dedication took place on 23 April 685. Inside the chancel are the Saxon aumbry (a pantry recess or wall cupboard), a simple chair thought to have been Bede's and the fifteenth century quire stalls while in the entrance stands an Anglo-Saxon wooden sculpture of Bede. Three small windows are set into the south wall of the chancel, the middle window containing Saxon glass made in the local monastic workshops is thought to be the oldest stained glass in Europe. It is said not to have been in the church originally and may have come from the monks' refectory.

Elsewhere in the north nave is a Saxon Cross with the inscription 'In this unique sign, life is restored to the world'. Outside on the south side are the ruined walls of some of the other buildings of the monastery dating from the eleventh century.

Although Jarrow is not the most convenient place to travel to nor St Paul's Church the easiest to find, a visit should nonetheless be on the itinerary of anyone visiting the area; the simplicity of the ancient building, its long history of Christian involvement, the story of Bede and the feeling that a visitor must get that they are walking in the footsteps of the earliest Christians, make going there overwhelmingly worthwhile.

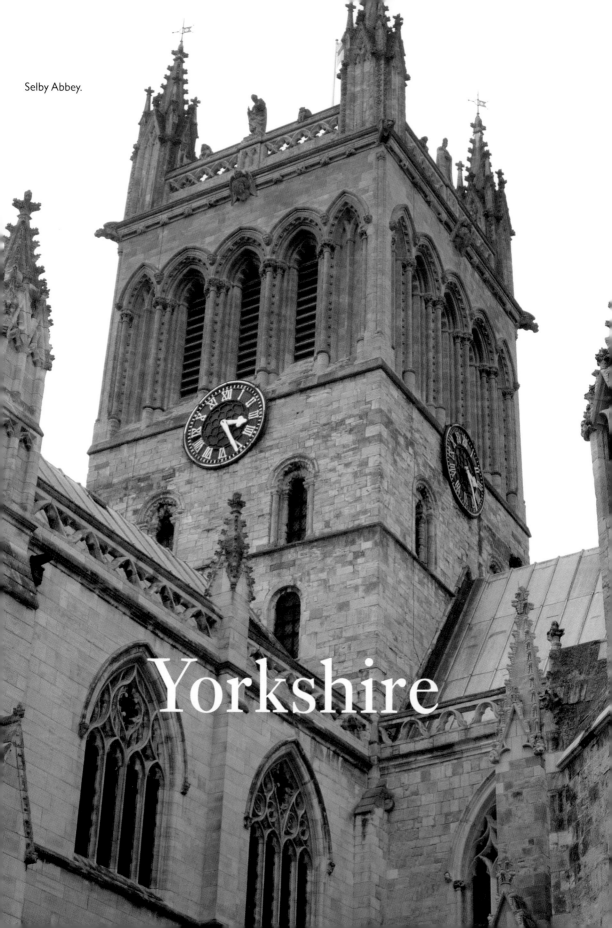

Selby Abbey.

Yorkshire

Chapter 12

East Riding of Yorkshire

■ Local railways in East Yorkshire ■ **Beverley Minster**
■ **Howden Minster** ■ **Bridlington Priory** ■

Getting There

The principal entry point by rail to East Yorkshire is through the city of Hull, travelling time from London currently being approximately three hours. York, a major junction on the East Coast mainline offering links to a wide variety of destinations can also be used, although the journey to destinations in East Yorkshire will involve a circuitous route via Selby.

The main rail artery within East Yorkshire is the line which runs from south to north from Hull to Scarborough via Beverley and Bridlington. Journey times are fifteen minutes from Hull to Beverley and forty-five minutes to Bridlington using the same train.

Howden has a station on the York to Hull line but is probably more easily reached by road.

Railway Notes

The East Riding is essentially an agricultural county, said to contain more livestock than people, and, prior to the Beeching cuts of the early 1960s, a network of branch lines carried produce from farm to market. Beginning in the nineteenth century, livestock, grain, potatoes, fruit, milk and wood from rural areas all came to be transported in bulk and as a result markets many miles distant could be reached in a matter of hours as opposed to days, as had been the case previously. However, as transport by road developed in the early twentieth century, rail's competitive advantage started to be lost. Road vehicles provided greater flexibility and time savings which could not be matched by trains and, while the Second World War saw the nation's railways provide a vital service without which the conflict could not have been won, the railways were worked to breaking point. A subsequent lack of infrastructure renewals and growing doubts over their long term utility, led inevitably to a programme of closures. Nowhere was this more marked than in the East Riding of Yorkshire.

Today, the county must rely upon a network of barely adequate roads to sustain its transport system. This situation applies not only in the rural hinterland but also in Hull, the major city of the region and a principal port, from where connections to the rest of Britain are inadequate by comparison with other centres of population. Thanks to private enterprise companies like Hull Trains, services to London have now been greatly improved and should improve further when, as expected, the main line is eventually electrified. Meanwhile, direct connections to other important centres in the provinces are also barely adequate except for the trans-Pennine route to Leeds, Manchester and beyond.

So what is the future for predominantly rural areas like East Yorkshire? Should they be left to live with inadequate communications provided mainly by road or are there other options?

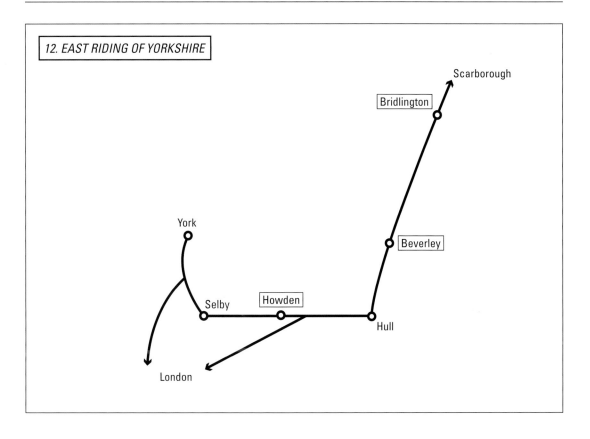

Campaigners have for some time been pressing to have certain former lines reinstated, most notably that which once connected York to Beverley and Hull, a route which would not only provide a useful freight link but also a passenger service to relieve an inadequate parallel trunk road. An initiative in the West Midlands now sees a single rail vehicle being used regularly on the branch line between Stourbridge and Stourbridge Junction. Called the Parry People Mover, it shuttles back and forth over a short distance to provide a dedicated link for a particular locality. Similar services have been provided in Germany as a means of serving isolated rural communities; might comparable schemes not be considered elsewhere in Britain? (See also Chapter 18).

As the previous chapter recounts, metro systems or tram trains in conurbations – integrated with local bus provision – and light railway systems in more rural areas are now real possibilities and examples abound across the country where imagination and clear thinking – to say nothing of the political willingness to relax financing restrictions – have brought improvements beyond their proponents' expectations. The recent extension of metro systems in cities like Manchester and Nottingham demonstrates the efficacy and popularity of such schemes and increasing numbers of local authorities are looking for ways to curb the unbridled use of the motor car in favour of rapid transport networks. It may sound fanciful but one day the human race may be forced to learn to do without the motor car as a personal carrier and accept other, centrally provided, means of 'smart' transport. Indeed this is already happening in our better organised cities in various ways.

Beverley Minster

A church which dominates the surrounding countryside and which is thought by many to be the most celebrated non-cathedral church in England. Thomas Becket is recorded as being the Provost 1153–1162 but may never have visited the Minster.

Admire the symmetry of the interior by standing by the west door and then walk east. Look for the 'musical' figures on the nave pillars, St John's tomb, the Snetzler organ, the misericords in the quire, the Percy tomb and the Coltman chair.

Over the centuries much has been written about Beverley Minster, its charm, its history, the dignity and detail of its fabric and its importance as a place of worship since its completion at the end of the fourteenth century. Matching many cathedrals in size and dominating the surrounding countryside, should there have ever been the requirement for a diocese in East Yorkshire, the minster would undoubtedly have been the bishop's seat. Today, it is the East Riding's premier church, the place to which Church and civic leaders naturally incline when required to represent their county.

Elsewhere in this book and its companion volume *English Cathedrals by Train*, mention will be found of the close links connecting the early churches at York, Ripon, Southwell and Beverley, all of which were founded or developed at similar times, involving some of the same early bishops. They were styled minsters, as were a number of other less well known churches in North East England, because their priests had a role in disseminating the gospel to people living in the surrounding areas at a time before parishes existed. Minster meant 'missionary centre' and, as explained in Chapter 3, minsters provided the base from where priests travelled around explaining Christianity and the bible to outlying communities in the days before parish churches came to be fully established

The Tower.

St John of Beverley commemorative plaque.

The nave. (Mervyn King)

The north side of the Minster.

Little is known about the early history of the church in Beverley. St Bede, in a record of the times, wrote that the area was sparsely inhabited when a monastery was founded there by a Bishop John in the early years of the eighth century. John has previously presided at Hexham and York after which he went to Beverley to retire. He was canonised St John of Beverley in 1037. After John came others, including King Athelstan and Archbishop Aelfric, but little is known of their churches except that St John's canonization and attributed miracles led to Beverley becoming a much visited centre of pilgrimage with beneficial consequences for the importance and economy of the town.

The present minster was started in the early thirteenth century. Beginning at the east end the chancel, the four transepts and the chapter house were all built in the Early English style. Much of the nave was then constructed in the first half of the fourteenth century in the Decorated style; however the north side of the nave west of the Highgate porch and the west end of the minster were completed later in the Perpendicular style; this break in continuity can be identified if you stand with your back to the second pillar on the north side of the nave and look across to its counterpart on the south side when you will see that they are not exactly aligned. Most of the church was thought to have been completed by 1400, although work would have undoubtedly continued thereafter.

Unlike the other two East Riding churches described in this chapter – Howden and Bridlington – both of which suffered terribly at the hands of Henry VIII's commissioners during the time

The nave and West Window.

of the Reformation, Beverley was relatively unscathed, although the buildings which supported its collegiate function, notably the Chapter House, were suppressed in 1548 and most of the minster's wealth confiscated by the Crown. Like so many other churches Beverley became the local parish church, a role it continues to discharge to this day.

The most logical way to view the interior is to begin in front of the great west door with its inside carvings of the four evangelists with their emblems beneath, and to look east. The door carvings were made around 1726 by Thornton of York, who also worked the ornate wooden Georgian cover above the Norman baptismal font of Frosterley marble located on the south side. Thornton, along with Nicholas Hawksmoor, worked collaboratively and did much work on the fabric of the church in the eighteenth century. Above the nave pillars are carvings of figures playing musical instruments; in medieval times Beverley was a centre for music in the same way as other places developed links with specific arts or skills and there are over seventy small 'musical' statues. Overall, the nave provides a marvellous aspect with the pillars rising to the *triforium* and above to the clerestory which allows light to flood into the church and provides a continuous line of vaulting east to the chancel. This surely is the view of the minster which will remain in most visitors' minds. The glass in the side aisles is Victorian as it is in most other windows of the building.

The original central tower had collapsed around 1213 and was not replicated in the present church, that part of the building being truncated at roof level. There is a boss in the centre

Revd Joseph Coltman's chair.

The Percy tomb on the north side of the High Altar.

of the tower ceiling which can be removed to allow materials to be hauled up into the roof space using a treadmill; no longer used for its original purpose the treadmill can be demonstrated to guided tours when the boss is removed from its setting. Below the tower is the nave altar, a round table installed in 1970 which, if necessary, can be moved to one side. To the west of the altar is a black slab set into the nave floor and inscribed with the details of St John of Beverley, covering the place where his remains are thought to be buried.

East of the nave altar is the late nineteenth century screen with the organ positioned above. The latter was built by Johann Snetzler between 1767 and 1769 and is considered to be one of his finest instruments with much of the original pipe work still in use today. Another of the minster's gems are the sixty-eight misericords beneath the seats in the 1520 quire, a number said to be greater than in any English cathedral. They depict animals and rural scenes. Beyond the quire lies the high altar which is divided from the Lady Chapel – now the retro-quire – and the east window by a reredos. The altar comprises a number of tiny figures including the twelve apostles in the centre. Statues, large and small, are very much a feature of Beverley Minster, both inside and outside, although the installation of many at the west front led to controversy in the past.

Immediately on the north side of the altar is the Percy Tomb built to commemorate Henry Percy, 4th Earl of Northumberland. The Percys were an assertive local family both in the East Riding where they lived at Leconfield Castle, and further north and would have been heavily involved in the affairs of the state during the fifteenth century. The 4th Earl was 'murdered by rebels' in 1489 following a 'disturbance at Topcliffe' in nearby North Yorkshire. Both the tomb of the 4th Earl and that of another Percy, Lady Eleanor, who died in 1328 and which stands in the same area, are said to be amongst the finest surviving examples of tombs of their time; another of the minster's treasures. To the north of the chancel in the side aisle can be seen the 'double' staircase which originally led to a chapter house, demolished after the Reformation. Another feature by the high altar is the Frith stool, the oldest possession of the minster, thought possibly to have been germane to the minster's prerogative to provide sanctuary to fugitives. *Frithu* is the Anglo-Saxon word for 'peace'.

There is much else to see in the church including some modern sculptures in the retro-quire reflecting on a 'theme of Spiritual and Artistic Pilgrimage', the east window – the glass of which is a collection of medieval pieces collected after a violent storm which did great damage – and the transepts. In the early eighteenth century, the north transept nearly collapsed and was only rescued by William Thornton, who contrived a massive wooden frame 'to push it back into position'; a pillar to the left of the minster shop entrance still shows a lean to the north. At the corner of the same transept in the nave side aisle are two memorials to former vicars who made notable contributions in providing money to support the education of poor children at the beginning of the nineteenth century; one was James Graves and the other Joseph Coltman. By all accounts, Coltman weighed 37 stone and needed a special chair to accommodate his bulk! The chair is now placed next to his memorial.

It would be wrong to leave Beverley without mentioning St Mary's Church, begun in the twelfth century and built in the English Gothic style, situated just to the south of the North Bar in the town and allegedly originally intended as a chapel to Beverley Minster. Of similar but different importance to the minster, St Mary's has its own treasures and Simon Jenkins in his book *England's Thousand Best Churches* says 'If Beverley had no Minster, St Mary's would still draw crowds to the town'. Happily, today the two churches work well together, each making its own contribution to local ministry and the furthering of the Church's work on earth.

Howden Minster

A Church dating back to Saxon times which grew in importance after the Norman Conquest under the direction of the Prince Bishops of Durham but then suffered serious decline in the reign of Henry VIII.

Look for the ruins at the east end, the truncated interior and the Saltmarshe Chantry which tells the story of one family long connected with the area.

Compared with its near neighbours – Beverley, Selby and Bridlington, all with their fine churches – Howden Minster is today but a shadow of what it was in medieval times. Once a thriving commercial centre, the town, close to the north bank of the river Ouse, is no longer the important place of the past. Before the eleventh century the church had links to Peterborough Abbey (now the cathedral) but these were severed in 1013 following a failure to pay danegeld, a land tax originally raised in the tenth century to buy peace from the Vikings. However, after the Norman Conquest fifty years later, events took a turn for the better when the powerful Prince Bishops of Durham ruled Howden-shire, as the local area was then known. The present church – today still styled a minster because of its importance as a religious centre in medieval times – was rebuilt in the thirteenth century. One of its earliest canons, John of Howden, a well-connected man of learning, came to be seen locally as a saint after his death in 1275.

The east end.

The tower of the minster today seen through the ruins of the original church.

A window in the Minster.

The Saltmarshe chantry.

The sixteenth century saw the end of Howden's time as a great religious centre. The disruption of Henry VIII's reign affected many churches and monasteries across the land but few more than Howden. First, the Pilgrimage of Grace in 1536, a Catholic-inspired rebellion by Yorkshire gentry led by Robert Aske against the king's plans to curb the powers of the Church – a rebellion which collapsed after a truce, the terms of which were not kept – and then the Reformation, led to the demise of Howden. The Prince Bishops withdrew to Durham and not long afterwards the quire of the minster was abandoned, its roof collapsing in 1609. The chancel vault also collapsed in 1696, as a result of which the east end of the minster was vacated.

Since the seventeenth century, worship has been confined to the west end, with the altar positioned under the crossing tower. The original stone *pulpitum* which once divided the two parts of the minster, now provides a reredos, the backcloth to the altar. To the east, the ruins of the chancel have been left as they were when the collapse occurred. They are now looked after by English Heritage.

There are several features to interest a visitor. Heraldic badges in the glass in the windows of the south nave aisle commemorate the families who assisted in the restoration of the church in the middle of the nineteenth century. Disaster struck more recently in 1929, when a fire started by arsonists in the area of the tower caused considerable damage. Much of the surrounding woodwork was destroyed but the opportunity was taken to restore the area as it was, Robert Thompson of Kilburn in North Yorkshire undertaking much of the work. His famous mouse carvings can be found in over thirty places in the restored woodwork. There are several theories as to why Thompson adopted the mouse as the emblem of his work, one being that his father warned him 'not to be as poor as a church mouse' Another has it that one of Thompson's carpenters once remarked that 'they were all as poor as church mice', whereupon he immediately carved one!

The west window is nineteenth century and was created by J B Capronnier, a Belgian glass worker also responsible for much of the stained glass in Cologne Cathedral in Germany. Another window of importance is that in the north transept commemorating the coronation of Elizabeth II, showing figures associated with the history of Howden. On the south side of the church is the Saltmarshe Chantry. An effigy of Sir Peter Saltmarshe, who lived from 1280 to 1338, is in the centre of the chantry and it told me a lot about the times in which he lived. Described as 'being of a turbulent and grasping disposition', he was challenged by the law on several occasions and imprisoned at least twice. He fought for Edward I against the Scots and apparently recovered his status as a nobleman, to eventually die an honoured and respected knight. In one corner of his chantry is a wooden coffin once used to transport bodies to the grave where, clothed only in a shroud, they were then tipped in and buried, the coffin then being returned to the church in preparation for its next assignment.

Bridlington Priory

Originally a large and influential priory church until the Reformation, since when its status has diminished and only the nave of the original building remains.

Look for the war memorials, the pulpit, discover the memorial to Sergeant Symon VC, find the Chapel of St John and the Eagle lectern and see how many of 'Mouseman' Thompson's mice you can find.

The original priory was built on the site of a Saxon church. Its founder, Walter de Gant, founded the Augustinian monastery in Bridlington in 1113 and it grew to become one of the largest houses of the order in Britain, owning land over a vast area of Yorkshire and influencing the lives of large numbers of people. In its heyday, the church building at the centre of the monastic settlement was over 400 feet long with transepts extending on both north and south sides measuring 150 feet in length. The location of the original south transept, relative to the present structure, is clearly marked on stone steps at the existing east end, outside the building. Locally, the priory church was said to be second only to York Minster in importance. Its central tower was surmounted by a crown spire, not unlike that which today graces Newcastle Cathedral.

St John of Bridlington, who died in 1379, was born nearby and rose to be the prior of the settlement. He was one of many important luminaries to serve the priory but the only one to be canonised. A number of miracles were attributed to him, the most publicised being when he is said to have saved the lives of five fishermen from Hartlepool in danger of drowning in the rough waters of the North Sea.

Models in the church show the extent of the original priory and the changes brought about by Henry VIII's programme of reform in the early and middle years of the sixteenth century. As with Howden Minster, a few miles to the south, the authorities at Bridlington were drawn into

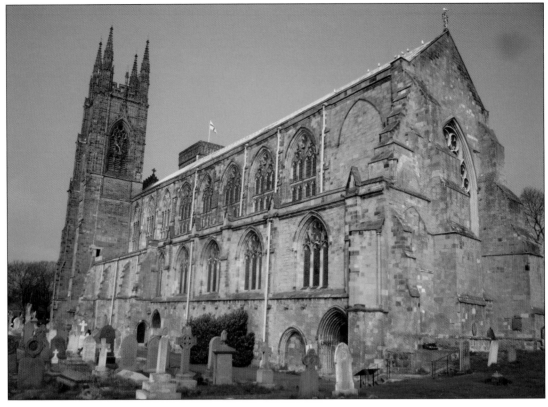

The east end today.

opposing the king and his plans and supported the Pilgrimage of Grace. The prior at the time, William Wood, was imprisoned in the Tower of London, tried and executed at Tyburn in 1537.

Following the end of the revolt, the king's commissioners surveyed the priory and destroyed all the monastic buildings other than the nave of the church and the priory gatehouse. The latter is called the Bayle and was subsequently used as a courthouse and prison for many years. The lead from the main roofs was stripped, the bells sold and much of the stone from demolished buildings transported to the local harbour to repair the wharves and quays, a responsibility the prior and his colleagues had apparently neglected. The destruction was brutal and the feelings of resentment must have been intense.

The remnants of the church, principally the original Gothic nave, became the local parish church which it remains to this day and is by any standards a very large building. The ten bays on either side of the nave rise to a *triforium* and clerestory where there is some stained glass; looking up it is easy to understand why comparisons might have been drawn between the priory and some cathedrals. The west end is dominated by two towers of different heights, added by George Gilbert Scott towards the end of the nineteenth century; according to details in the church they were constructed 'to make the Church more inspiring and to carry a peal of bells'. They certainly confer a sense of dignity on the truncated building despite their being unbalanced.

The west window is said to be one of the largest in England while the east window, installed in 1861 to replace two former windows originally recycled from the demolished chancel in 1538, is a

The West window – one of the largest in the North of England.

Tree of Jesse. On the south side of the nave is the Founder's Stone, a slab of Tournai marble which it is thought may cover Walter de Gant's burial place. Close by is a memorial to George Symons, a holder of a Victoria Cross won at Inkerman on 6th June 1855 during the Crimean War. Symons, a sergeant in the Royal Artillery, showed exceptional courage when he stormed an enemy gun battery, knocking out the guns, enabling a successful allied attack. Symons died at Bridlington in 1871.

The north side of the nave.

The pulpit.

The history of the priory and its decline is well told within today's church with plenty of explanations of historical and contemporary facts, all of which make it such an interesting place to visit. One of the most prominent features in the north west corner of the church are the war memorials from two world wars; positioned close together they show in stark detail the contribution to the fighting made by Bridlington and its surrounding villages and the extent of the loss of life of men destined never to return. At a time when the nation is marking anniversaries of both world wars, their sacrifice makes for sober contemplation.

These descriptions of three widely different but historically important churches in East Yorkshire are but a foretaste for anybody interested in discovering the county's many parish churches, scattered as they are across sparsely populated countryside, each containing its own treasures. Sadly most are only occasionally visited by the outside world today.

A view from the South West. Note the different height of the towers.

The war memorial.

Chapter 13

North Yorkshire

■ The Selby avoiding line ■ Some observations on overseas rail travel
■ **Selby Abbey** ■

Getting There

Originally Selby lay on the main East Coast route from London to Scotland at the spot where the river Ouse is crossed by a swing bridge. In the late 1960s the development of an extensive drift coalmine between York and Selby led to the closure of a section of the railway to the north of the town in order to avoid areas of mining subsidence and the subsequent building of a replacement line to the west. As a result, Selby is now principally connected by trains travelling from King's Cross to Hull, taking approximately two hours to reach the town. An alternative is to travel from London to York and to then take a local train to Selby using the diversionary route, overall timings being not dissimilar.

Railway Notes

When completed, the East Coast diversionary route was the longest section of new railway built since the nineteenth century, now surpassed by the HS1 route from the Channel Tunnel to London. Approximately twenty-five miles in length it carried the main line away from areas of potential subsidence while, at the same time, removing the need for train movements to be suspended every time the Selby Swing Bridge needed to be rotated to allow the passage of river traffic. Given the growing frequency of railway traffic in recent years, some solution would have had to have been found to avoid the unacceptability of frequent main line disruption, regardless of the problems posed by potential subsidence.

Train travel abroad has become increasingly popular in recent years, both as a viable way for business people to access continental destinations and as a pleasant means of undertaking a journey to an overseas holiday resort. A parallel development in the leisure market has also led to the creation of luxury foreign rail-based holidays in countries like Canada, America and India as well as in parts of South America and South East Asia. Indeed, there is today hardly an area of the globe accessible by rail where an enterprising tour operator has not devised a route to attract the train tourist.

European rail services are usually compared favourably to their British counterparts; they are seen to be more efficient, cleaner and invariably more punctual. While such comparisons may often be well founded overall, they are not always fair nor indeed accurate, especially when those commenting themselves travel very little overseas and, when they do, only travel on modern trains along high speed lines. On the whole, British trains have faster schedules than their Continental counterparts, while foreign rural services can often be very poorly managed. However, sleek, well operated express services conveying passengers to a wide variety of destinations across and

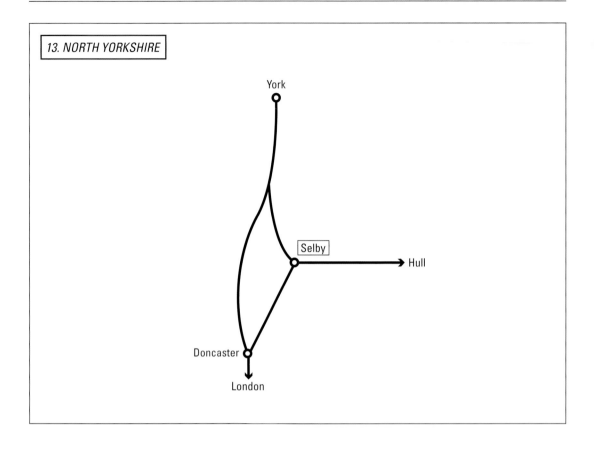

13. NORTH YORKSHIRE

York

Selby

Hull

Doncaster

London

beyond European borders, can be captivating, leaving an impression that European nations have discovered how to run efficient services while Britain has not. Safety is another area assessed by those drawing comparisons between nations' railways and here Britain certainly has the edge, a recent survey stating unequivocally that Britain has the best record in Europe.

Long distance rail travel, including in overnight sleeper trains, can be a pleasant experience and considerably more restful than flying or driving on traffic clogged motorways. For instance, trains crossing the continent in a day or less, for example from Copenhagen to Zurich or Paris to Rome, invoke memories of the twentieth century Orient Express from London to Istanbul. While modern rolling stock is well designed and comfortable, catering is however not of the standard that used to apply in a more leisurely age.

The efficiency of the principal trans-European expresses has to be acknowledged, as my own recent experience showed. Travelling through the Channel tunnel and then to Vienna through Germany, later returning the length of Austria before catching a French TGV (*Train Grand Vitesse*) from Zurich, was certainly a most enjoyable experience and demonstrated the best and the least good aspects of Continental train travel. Modern rolling stock, efficiently operated, pertinent electronically delivered train information – both on stations and on board – and courteous staff were much in evidence but schedules were not taxing, fares expensive, trains not immune from running late and help for perplexed passengers at large stations sometimes non-existent. We should not allow ourselves to labour under an inferiority complex that British services are generally of a lesser standard than those of their Continental cousins; they are not.

146

Inter City Europe.

A French TGV from Brittany to Paris.

North Eastern Railway tank engine on the turntable at the NRM, York.

Cut away depiction of a steam locomotive at the NRM, York.

Selby Abbey

An abbey church with a long and interesting history and an important role today in the Diocese of York.

Look for the Norman pillars in the nave and how the style changes as you proceed west, the windows in both transepts recording the story of Benedict and the grant of a charter to build the abbey in 1069, the High Stewards' stalls in the quire and the 'squint' in the north quire aisle.

The town of Selby lies approximately fifteen miles south of York and on a clear day York Minster can be seen from the tower of the abbey. The town is said to have got its name from linking the Saxon word sele meaning 'willow copse' with the Viking word by for a 'town' to give the name 'Seleby.'

It was there in about 1069 that Benedict, a Frenchman, arrived after a visit to Auxerre Abbey in Southern France where legend has it he was commanded to found an abbey at 'Seleby' in England. This instruction apparently came in a vision from St Germain, a nobleman living in the early part of the fifth century, who, in his short life had been a soldier, later converting to

The heraldic arms of two recent High Stewards.

The west front.

Christianity and being appointed a bishop. The story of his life and his instruction to Benedict is depicted in the north transept window of today's abbey. Legend has it that Benedict recognised the site he had been instructed to find when three swans landed on the river Ouse. Three swans mounted on a heraldic shield have remained the abbey and the town coat of arms ever since.

In 1069, William I was in York subduing the remaining northern communities still hostile to Norman rule and the opportunity was taken to seek his permission for the building of a church at Selby, a charter to do so being given the following year. A wooden abbey was quickly constructed, Benedict was ordained as the first Abbot and those men recruited into the abbey were enrolled into the Rule of St Benedict, a set of commandments introduced into England in the sixth century which stipulated strict rules to be observed by adherents to the order.

Benedict was succeeded as abbot by Hugh in 1097. Hugh was a master builder and quickly determined to construct a more permanent abbey which he began in 1100, handling much of the work himself. The resulting church was built using magnesian limestone which came from a quarry at Monk Fryston; a seam of the stone runs from near Tadcaster to the north of Selby and in a southerly direction towards Doncaster and still provides the stone for York Minster as well as the abbey.

The early nave of Hugh's church was finished after about a hundred years. Some pillars at the eastern end soon showed signs of buckling following subsidence, no doubt caused by the site being so close to the river and despite Hugh's close attention to the need for reinforced foundations in

The view over Selby looking west.

The quire.

an area of high water table. The second nave pillar on the south side is decorated with a diamond pattern similar to the pillars in Durham Cathedral from where Hugh had come to Selby. That pillar is called Abbot Hugh's pillar and the early part of the nave reflects work previously done at Durham. As the nave was extended west, the style of construction changed from Romanesque to Early English and later a *triforium* and clerestory were added, the latter to allow light into the nave. Overall most of the work in the nave is twelfth century, although alterations have been made since.

Over the following years, work progressed under a succession of abbots. After 1280, the quire was enlarged and the east window installed. Similar to many other churches of the period, the window portrays Christ's family tree in vivid colours and with most of the figures identifiable from an accompanying chart. Above the Jesse window in the tracery is a depiction of St Michael weighing souls on the day of judgement. Lower down, two small panels show the Royal coat of arms to the right while the town's arms are in an equivalent position to the left. It has been suggested that this places the town's arms on the heavenward side of the window while those of the royal family are on the 'doomed side'.

The stalls in the quire are decorated with the arms of some of the abbey's High Stewards. The appointment of High Steward was an ancient office predating the Reformation when it was abolished, but reintroduced in 1974. High Stewards were traditionally important local people under whose patronage the abbey existed and to whom the abbot could turn in times of need.

Like so many churches of its time, Selby Abbey has suffered its fair share of disasters over a long life. Two particular events in the first years of the sixteenth century would have dominated the lives of Yorkshire people; notwithstanding that Selby Abbey might not have taken an active role in the Pilgrimage of Grace uprising in 1536, it would undoubtedly have been affected by the outcome. Many of the revolution's ring leaders were tried, convicted and brutally executed in nearby York, their shattered bodies left on display hanging from the city's gates for months or years afterwards in order to deter further opposition to Tudor rule. Royal retribution was swift and cruel, although the last abbot of Selby was spared the axe. The second event, soon afterwards, was of course the Dissolution of the monasteries in Yorkshire and elsewhere, Selby Abbey meeting its fate in December 1539 when the monastic settlement was terminated leaving only the abbey church and a gatehouse to be used by parishioners.

The civil war of 1642 heaped more problems on the church which was by then being used for local worship, with Sir Thomas Fairfax leading the Commonwealth troops in defence of the town. However, Charles I's forces also occupied the area and billeted men and stabled horses in the church. In 1690, the upper part of the tower collapsed, severely damaging the south transept and part of the quire; temporary repairs were made but it was not until the latter part of the nineteenth century that Sir George Gilbert Scott carried out a complete restoration of the nave, to be followed in 1890 by John Oldrid Scott who repaired the damaged tower, in the process reducing it in height to diminish its weight on unstable foundations.

A far worse disaster struck in October 1906 when the roof timbers of the quire caught fire, gutting most of the interior and destroying the quire screen and all of the wooden fixtures in the quire and chancel. Nothing daunted, the people of Selby determined to repair the damage and immediately set out to raise the necessary money. John Oldrid Scott was appointed to carry out the rebuilding and within three years both the nave and quire were again in use. The final act in the long programme to safeguard the abbey church came in 1935 when Charles Marriot Oldrid Scott increased the height of the western towers to a position similar to their original construction.

As noted earlier, the window in the north transept tells the story of St Germain and his instructions to Benedict to select the site of the original abbey; meanwhile the south transept window records those involved in the granting of land for the monastery including William I, his wife Queen Matilda, shown holding the infant Henry I, St Germain and Benedict. A display cabinet in the transept contains details of the visit of Elizabeth II in 1969 when, accompanied by the Duke of Edinburgh, she visited Selby to celebrate the beginning of the church's tenth century and to disburse the Royal Maundy, the first time that annual ceremony was held other than in a cathedral.

There is much else to see in the abbey. Some of the bays of the south chancel aisle contain columns, the capitals of which were carved by Tom Strudwick, with several showing animals such as deer, rabbits and calves. You will have to look carefully to find them. There is another capital in the corresponding north aisle which, within the carving, contains a miniature sculpted head of Edward VII. A torch is provided so that you can illuminate the interior. A few steps to the west on the aisle wall there is a 'squint' which would have allowed those on the periphery of the church to observe what was happening during services in the chancel., similar to the squints in the west window at Great Malvern Priory. Some contend that the inclusion of a squint in a church indicated the presence of lepers who were unclean and therefore forbidden to attend services in person, but whether Selby ever had any lepers is uncertain.

A demonstration of how a squint might have been used.

High up in the south clerestory of the quire is a window containing a shield representing the Washington family; the design is of three red stars above two red horizontal stripes against a white background. The window is thought to originate from a connection with John Wessington, Prior of Durham in the early fifteenth century; the links between Durham and Selby have already been highlighted from the time of Abbot Hugh. However, more intriguing is that there may have been a link between Wessington and George Washington, a descendant and the first American President. There is speculation that the Wessington arms as shown in the window could have been used by Washington as the basis for the American Stars and Stripes flag. The connection is explained in a leaflet in the abbey.

Well explained in its guide book and today beautifully cared for, Selby Abbey is a joy to visit. Despite a series of major disasters and past years of decline which other communities might have found it hard to survive, the church stands today as fitting a testimony as any to the Christian purpose for which it was originally built. I visited on a lovely April day to be shown around and was received with the greatest courtesy.

Chapter 14

West Yorkshire

■ Pacers, railcars and urban networks ■ **Leeds Minster**
■ **Halifax Minster** ■

Railway Notes

Pacer rail buses were first introduced by British Rail in the 1980s. The design was conceived as a low cost train primarily suitable for use on rural and suburban rail routes. Originally intended as a short term solution to resolve a rolling stock shortage, the trains are still to be found in service although their inability to provide suitable access for disabled passengers means that they must soon be withdrawn from service if they are not to breach accessibility regulations, due to be enforced in 2020. The description 'short term' gives an indication of the fragmented approach to the procurement of railway rolling stock pertaining in the years before privatisation in the late 1990s. Travel by train was generally accorded a low priority by Government and this was reflected in inadequate funding and a policy seemingly designed to provide a minimum level of resourcing, the more so on short distance suburban rail networks. Is it any wonder that many passengers abandoned rail transport at the time and might well do so again unless more congenial replacements can soon be acquired?

The original Pacers are now over thirty years old and provide a poor advertisement for passenger transport in the present era. The concept of 'a bus on rails' does not fit the improving image of more modern rolling stock now being introduced and recent campaigns in the media directed at hastening the Pacers' withdrawal have resulted in ministerial promises of early replacement, although it is unclear when. Communities in the North of England, in particular those in West Yorkshire and Lancashire, have sustained travel by Pacer for generations and now deserve better.

What is wrong with the Pacer? Apart from the fact that a bus chassis design does not lend itself to transfer into a rail vehicle, the fixed four wheel two axle configuration makes for an uncomfortable ride, especially when a train is travelling at speed, around curves or over points. A bogie might have resolved these problems. The interior of the trains is austere, strictly functional with hard

155

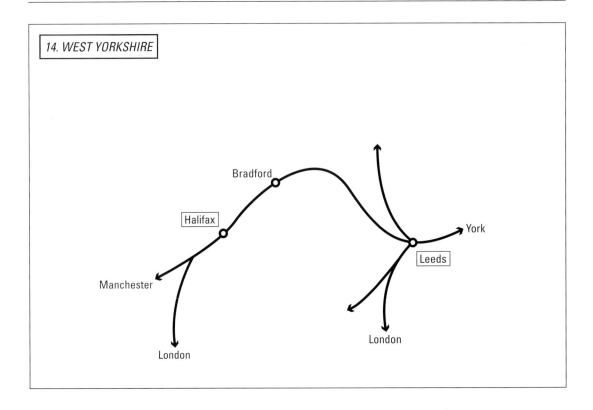

14. WEST YORKSHIRE

A pacer railcar.

A Grand Central 'open access' service from London leaving Halifax.

bench seats like a bus. Not for nothing are the vehicles labelled 'nodding donkeys' by those who must use them regularly; some people have even claimed they cause nausea. Acceleration is slow and entry to and exit from the vehicles is difficult for those with luggage. New stock is being designed to replace the Pacer but this will take time to materialise; meanwhile it is expected that more comfortable diesel trains cascaded from routes soon to be electrified elsewhere, might be used as short term replacements.

The whole issue of urban commuter networks is currently under review. Following government led initiatives the London Overground network – originally some of British Rail's former surface routes in the capital – has now been placed under the aegis of the Mayor of London and has been a real success for the better services which have resulted. Elsewhere, in some of our larger cities the quality of urban transport is now improving since individual local authorities were granted wider powers to plan and co-ordinate local provision. This is touched upon in Chapter 11 where the development of the Tyne and Wear Metro is described. The Liverpool city region is another example where local transport provision has been modernised, especially the rail network. Progress in other places is now long overdue and it is to be expected that the empowering of local authorities to spend funds for their communities through bodies like Transport for the North or individual Passenger Transport Authorities, will soon improve both the image and utility of local commuter services and the lot of those who have no alternative but to use them.

Leeds Minster

An urban church dating from 1841, although a place of worship has probably existed on the site for centuries.

Look for the mosaics at the east end, Sally Scott's Angel Screen and the tiny statue of Rev Geoffrey Studdert Kennedy.

There are many churches in Leeds, several dedicated to St Peter. Leeds Minster, the official parish church, is close to the city centre and about ten minutes' walk from the station. It is surrounded by new roads designed to speed traffic flows through the commercial quarter of the city and, like so many city centre churches, it stands rather forlornly, seemingly isolated from those who might wish to worship there.

The present church is relatively new. In 1837, plans were being drawn up to give the building a major overhaul but the existing structure was found to be in such a poor state that it was decided that total reconstruction was necessary. The recently appointed vicar, the Rev Walter Hook, took the opportunity to build a church more in keeping with the demands of a growing city, an aspiration neatly fitting his own determination to reach out to a wide range of new worshippers. His perception was that a church should be 'a place of perfection where fine music enhanced dignified worship, surrounded by colour and good design.' The result was an imposing building, capable of holding 1600 people.

Leeds Minster east end.

The interior of the church.

The earlier structures, of which few vestiges remain, probably went back to the seventh or eighth century when a church was first believed to have been established near a crossing on the river Aire. This early church was recorded by William I in the Domesday Book in 1086 but what transpired thereafter is not clearly chronicled, other than that St Peter's for a long time served a vast area of the growing city and was always looked upon as the mother church of the urban centre.

The church is rather dark inside but there is plenty to see. The east end, which was altered between 1870 and 1880, is dominated by glass, some of which was collected on the continent; below the window and surrounding the reredos and high altar are mosaics made of marble and alabaster. They were derived from work by Salviatis of Venice and were made by George Street and represent the apostles with St Paul and St Barnabas. A few feet away on the south side of the chancel is a tenth century cross which has been pieced together from relics discovered on the site of the present church.

Memorials abound to former vicars or prominent Leeds citizens. The pulpit and the organ occupy a position on the south side by the crossing, the pulpit's heavy Gothic style emphasising its purpose as a place from where the word of God was to be pronounced and listened to in silence! Opposite above the north door is the Angel Screen: based upon the story of Jacob's ladder, it was designed by Sally Scott and given to the church in 1998 by Lord Marshall, a recent generous benefactor. On the south side of the nave is a charming miniature statue of Geoffrey Studdert

Atomic test programme memorial.

Kennedy, an acclaimed First World War chaplain dubbed 'Woodbine Willie' for the manner in which he approached and supported soldiers in the trenches throughout the war. He later became a strong supporter of the ideas promoted by the Industrial Christian Fellowship and 'Tubby' Clayton in the inter war years; there is also a memorial to him in Worcester Cathedral.

Located at the east end of the churchyard and with little adornment is a memorial to those who took part – including presumably those who lost their lives – in the atomic test programme in the Pacific Ocean in the 1950s . Little has been made official as to what happened during the tests or their effectiveness but they were clearly part of a project of great national importance. Why Leeds Parish Church (as it then was) should have been chosen as the location for such a low key memorial must remain a mystery, certainly to me. Montebello, Maralinga and Christmas Island are all places recorded on the memorial along with other locations where tests were presumably held.

St Peter's Church was first styled a Minster in 2012. Following the amalgamation of the dioceses of Bradford, Wakefield and Ripon into a single diocese of Leeds and the Dales, incorporating the areas covered by those three former dioceses, St Peter's has assumed the role of the bishop's church although whether a *cathedra* or throne is to be installed for him is not known. What role the cathedrals of the three former dioceses will undertake in the new arrangement is also unclear, although it is understood that bishops will continue to be appointed to each and the churches will continue as centres of local worship.

Halifax Minster

Another recently styled minster with a rich local history and important connections to an army regiment.

Look for the painted roof with its coat of arms, the Duke of Wellington's regimental chapel and 'Old Tristram' near the entrance.

Halifax was once an industrial town famous amongst other enterprises for the manufacture of carpets. Located in a series of valleys, during the Industrial Revolution the smoke from its many factories never really cleared above street level where even today the houses still show the results of many years exposure to smoke and soot. The ashlar stones of St John's Church, since 2009 styled Halifax Minster, give a similar appearance. However the town is a much cleaner, brighter place today. The church is less than three hundred yards from the station.

A church in the twelfth century was replaced by the present building around 1438; sections of the north wall are believed to be Norman, it being possible to make out some typical 'zig zag' patterns which could have originated from that period. Similar to Leeds Minster, the church is quite dark inside, although both the east window, given by a local industrialist in 1856, and the window in the Wellington Chapel to its right, add considerable brightness to that end of

The view of the minster from the east end.

The east window based upon a design from the Great Exhibition of 1851.

Duke of Wellington's Regimental Chapel.

the building. Halifax has been the regimental home of the Duke of Wellington's Regiment, now a battalion of The Yorkshire Regiment following the Army's regimental amalgamations of the 1990s, for a more than a hundred years. The Wellington Chapel has been dedicated to the 'Dukes' since 1951 and several regimental colours are laid up there. Some of the clear glass windows in the chapel are amongst a number throughout the building which were given by Nathaniel Waterhouse after the destruction of the previous stained glass during the civil war in the mid seventeenth century – they are described as the Commonwealth windows.

Originally, the pews in the nave would have been of a high sided box construction dating from the 1630s, but George Gilbert Scott lowered them in 1878 when he undertook various redevelopments. Chapels, tombs and the decoration on the roof of the nave and chancel reflect some of the vicars who have ministered to the people of Halifax over the centuries. The ninety-two panels of the roof are painted with the coat of arms of the first thirty vicars, along with those of local families, whilst others depict the twelve tribes of Judah. Meanwhile, the Holdsworth Chapel commemorates Robert Holdsworth, the vicar for ten years from 1525. He had the misfortune to become involved in a feud between two local families – the Tempests and the Saviles – and was murdered by supporters of the former.

There is a memorial in the south west corner of the church to Bishop Ferrer – born in Halifax – who served as Bishop of St David's during the reign of Henry VIII but was later executed by his daughter, Mary, following the death of her brother Edward VI, when Bishop Ferrer opposed her decision to take England back to Roman Catholicism. One of his contemporaries in the first years of the sixteenth century and a one-time vicar of Halifax – William Rokeby – also achieved high archiepiscopal status when he went to be Archbishop of Dublin; his heart is said to be buried in the church in a lead box.

The William and Mary altar rails, the fifteenth century font cover, once brightly painted, which had to be hidden during the time of the Commonwealth, and 'Old Tristram', a wooden effigy of a beggar near the entrance to the church who was licensed to beg outside in the late 1600s in order to raise funds to help the poor, are amongst other treasures in the building and all bear testimony to the role and importance of St John's over the last six hundred years.

Both the churches reviewed in this chapter have recently been accorded the status of a minster by Archbishop John Sentamu of York. In conferring the title of minster on both Leeds and Halifax churches the Archbishop and his bishops would no doubt have had in mind the need to stimulate support for the church and to encourage fresh engagement by the latter in the civic life of the towns and cities where it is located. In discharging such a role, there can be little difference between the task once performed by York or Beverley Minsters in medieval times and that now given fresh impetus by the conferment of similar status on the principal churches in Leeds and Halifax.

Chesterfield, the twisted spire.

East Midlands

Chapter 15

Derbyshire

■ Further electrification of the railways ■ **The 'Crooked Spire' Church, Chesterfield**
■ George Stephenson's burial place ■

Getting There

Chesterfield, a town of more than a hundred thousand people, lies about twenty minutes south of Sheffield on the Midland main line connecting London to South Yorkshire. The journey time from St Pancras is about one hour and fifty minutes and trains are frequent. Chesterfield is also well connected to other major centres in the North of England via Sheffield.

Railway Notes

For many years the Government's plans to electrify Britain's railways have lagged behind similar schemes initiated by her continental neighbours. During the latter half of the twentieth century the only major long distance routes in Britain to be converted to electrical traction were the east and west coast main lines from London to Scotland and the Great Eastern main lines into East Anglia. Earlier 'third rail' electrification of most of the Southern Railway and

East Midlands trains pass at Chesterfield en route to and from London.

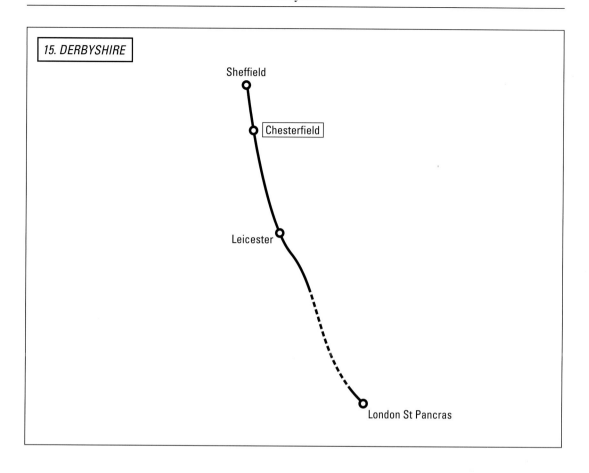

15. DERBYSHIRE

Sheffield

Chesterfield

Leicester

London St Pancras

some urban transit systems had been completed before the Second World War, but little else had been done. Indeed one principal freight route, utilising electrical power and running across the Pennines from Sheffield to Manchester via the Woodhead Tunnel, had even been closed in the 1960s. In retrospect, it seems strange that at a time when steam locomotives were being replaced by cleaner and more efficient forms of traction, the emphasis should have been on diesel power and not electrical. Today, the agenda points firmly towards electrification as the most efficient and economic power source for the future as the current Government's forward plans demonstrate.

Scope for further electrification had therefore existed for several decades and new schemes began to be approved in the first years of the twenty-first century; even so many projects have been started piecemeal – often for reasons of financial expediency – although it has always been recognised that, in order to achieve the full benefits of modernisation, they would eventually need to be completed in their entirety. Such a short term approach to the planning and implementation of capital schemes has always tended to be a weakness inherent in the British approach to new investment. As a result, projects can take an inordinate length of time to come to fruition.

Today, the wiring of the Great Western main line from London to Bristol and Swansea and the Midland main line from St Pancras to Nottingham and Sheffield are either underway or planned while a number of shorter routes in the North West and Yorkshire are set to follow; other schemes are further off in the planning process. There is also an embryo plan to constitute a trunk freight route up 'the spine of England' to carry electrically hauled freight traffic from Southampton

High speed electrification: the East Coast mainline at Grantham.

docks to Leeds, to move imports and exports more efficiently around the country. Meanwhile, the High Speed Two railway is set to revolutionise passenger transport although it will not come to fruition until 2030 at the earliest. Further north in Scotland, the devolved Scottish Government has pursued a policy of upgrading a number of lines, although not all will use electrical power, to reopen old railway lines or provide additional commuter routes to major centres. If even half of all these plans are achieved Britain could eventually have a transport system fit for the twenty first century.

So, what are the benefits of electrical traction? In a nutshell, cleaner technology, greater reliability, more seats on trains and better sustainability. Electrical traction with motors placed beneath carriages can create extra seats since no locomotive is required; electric power sources accelerate and decelerate quicker and require less maintenance than their diesel counterparts. On average it costs around 60p per mile to sustain a diesel train as compared to 40p for a train on an electrified line. Fuel costs are less, as is the wear and tear on the track. Carbon dioxide emissions are also less.

Britain does not compare well with its continental neighbours when progress in modernising transport networks is assessed. All Switzerland's principal operational rail routes are electrified; seventy per cent in Sweden and sixty nine per cent in Germany. Britain is towards the bottom of the European league with only forty per cent.

St Mary and All Saints Church, Chesterfield

The 'Crooked Spire' Church.

Look for the twisted spire, the Norman font and the brightly coloured and distinctive anniversary window.

A manufacturing town on the edge of the Peak District, Chesterfield's origins go back to Roman times. Its principal church, located within easy walking distance of the railway station, dates from the fourteenth century, although considerable changes to the interior of the building were made in Victorian times. An earlier church was said to have been founded in the time of Edward the Confessor in the eleventh century, while the growing prosperity of the town was confirmed in King John's reign when he granted a charter.

The east end of today's parish church was begun in the thirteenth century, followed by construction of the four pillars of the tower, dedicated in 1234. The main areas of the church were all completed by about 1360. However, more work was carried out around 1500, when the roof was raised to its present level and the clerestory was added, with a reconstruction of the west end completed by the middle of the sixteenth century. Further rebuilding took place in the eighteenth and again in the nineteenth century when George Gilbert Scott carried out some internal re-ordering and added more glass. Even so, a report delivered by the local rural dean in May 1887 and recorded in the church guide book, was critical of the general state of the fabric; quotes such as 'the Chancel very dilapidated'; 'poor ventilation' and 'the linen poor and shabby' – all summed up by the phrase 'the church is fast going to decay.' painted a picture of general disenchantment. As a result, further improvements were carried on into the next century.

However, the church's main claim to fame must be the manner in which its spire has tilted over a number of years. Added in the fourteenth century, the spire has twisted into a 'corkscrew' shape: it rises to a height of 228 feet and today leans eight and a half feet to the south and nearly four feet to the west. Its strange configuration is often compared with the phenomenon of the leaning tower of Pisa in Italy. Its distorted shape can be seen from many directions and from some distance, including by those journeying through the area by rail.

There are several theories as to the shape of the spire. The most probable is that the heat of the sun on green timbers caused one of the principal supports to split resulting in the spire gradually tilting and 'bulging'. When this occurred is unknown. The spire is clad with lead plates laid in 'herring bone' fashion, something which emphasises its extraordinary shape. History has it that at one time the spire was declared to be unsafe and should be demolished but the people of the town were unwilling to allow that to happen and consequently strengthened it. When floodlit, the spire presents a ghostly impression.

Other less convincing explanations for the spire's shape abound; that Lucifer whilst flying from Nottingham to Sheffield alighted briefly on the spire and sneezed thereby twisting the structure while another suggests that a beautiful maiden, a bride to be, entered the church to be married whereupon the spire bowed down in admiration.

The interior of the church verges on the gloomy, the mainly Victorian glass tending to restrict the light which penetrates, but the nave is wide and elegant and there are five chapels clustered towards the east end, each with its own adornments. The nave is built in the Decorated style, with the uppermost arches in the clerestory being Perpendicular. The great west window was created

The twisted spire.

The 'Joshua' window.

The 750th anniversary window 1984.

in 1890 by Hardman and portrays the life of Joshua. Further east, the nave altar, used for the principal services, was built in the 1940s while the screen behind shows four kings – Edward the Confessor, Henry III, Richard II and George VI – in whose reigns there took place notable events in the life of the church.

The south transept has as its centre the baptismal font, the oldest fixture in the church, possibly dating from before the Norman Conquest. It was apparently taken out of the church at some stage and was not restored to its rightful place until 1898, when it was dug up in the vicarage garden. The Lady Chapel is unusually wide and includes a collection of tombs of the Foljambe family, important Derbyshire squires from the sixteenth century. To the left of the altar is a brass plate commemorating Geoffrey Clayton, vicar for ten years from 1924, who later became Archbishop of Cape Town. The east window depicting the Creed dates from 1947 and was designed by Christopher Webb.

Amongst the more recent glass is the Anniversary window in the south nave aisle, given by the people of Chesterfield in 1984 to mark the church's 750th anniversary. The bright colours and easily identifiable depictions in the window trace the history of the town from the eleventh century to the present. The principal historical events are covered: social and industrial change; the arrival of the railway as well as more modern recent developments and of course the Crooked Spire Church itself. At the top is the shield of the diocese of Derby, symbolic of 'the Church

The font, the oldest fixture in the church, it possibly pre-dates the Conquest.

body'. The window provides a fascinating and instructive view of a town whose foremost church has worked closely with the civic authorities and townspeople over many years to the benefit of all.

In 1961, a disastrous fire in the north transept did great damage, including destroying the Snetzler organ, two hundred years old and one of the few of that construction remaining in Britain at the time. The fire was thought to have started due to an electrical fault in the organ. Undaunted, the church authorities purchased a replacement which was in place two years later.

Finally there is a local verse in the church guide books which offers a tongue in cheek explanation for the state of the spire:

'Whichever way you turn your eye
It always seems to be awry
Pray can you tell the reason why?
The only reason known of weight
Is that the thing was never straight.'

Railway Notes

Another church in the town is Holy Trinity where George Stephenson is buried in the chancel. In 1837 the railway pioneer settled in Chesterfield for the last ten years of his life, living at Tapton House to the north of the town. Holy Trinity is about half a mile from the Crooked Spire church and contains a memorial window given by George's son Robert. Meanwhile there is a more recent statue to Stephenson outside the railway station. See Chapter 11 for more details of George Stephenson and the development of early railways on Tyneside, for many of which he was responsible.

The recent Statue of George Stevenson outside Chesterfield station.

Boston, The Stump.

Eastern England

Black & white montage of Crewe in the 1950s.

(Taken by Tony Storey.

Chapter 16

Lincolnshire

■ Railway towns ■ Crewe
■ St Botolph's Church, Boston (The Stump) ■

Getting There

The communities of coastal Lincolnshire have always relied more on the sea than on land routes for their trade and Boston at the southern end of the county is no exception. Travel from London King's Cross involves an hour's journey on the East Coast mainline to Grantham, with a change there into a train to Boston, which will require approximately a further fifty minutes travel depending upon the number of stations called at. Alternatively, the journey can be made from either Doncaster to the north, involving a change at Lincoln and Sleaford, or from Peterborough to the south with a change at Sleaford only; journey times will be considerably longer than via Grantham since trains may not connect.

Railway Notes

As railways developed in the nineteenth century and spread their tentacles across the country, a number of communities were selected as centres for the construction and development of the accompanying railway industries. Changed almost overnight from small rural villages into sprawling industrial workshops, these railway towns became the hubs which allowed the extraordinary expansion of railway routes in the period between 1830 and the end of that century. Eventually, each of the 'big four' railway companies created by act of parliament in 1923 had its own company town or towns, where locomotives and rolling stock were built and from where the infrastructure to create a comprehensive railway network was planned and managed.

Swindon in Wiltshire was selected by Brunel to be the Great Western 'home' while Doncaster and Darlington emerged as the towns where most of the London and North Eastern locomotives would be built. On the other side of the country, Crewe in Cheshire and Derby were selected by the London and North Western and Midland railway companies respectively, both being retained when those two companies amalgamated to form the London Midland and Scottish Railway in 1923. Meanwhile, Eastleigh in Hampshire and Brighton serviced the profusion of short distance lines which were later to form the Southern Railway, while St Rollox in Glasgow was a principal base for many railway companies originating in Scotland. Other smaller centres also played a part, for example Horwich in Manchester and Inverurie near Aberdeen.

Most of these towns served a railway purpose for well over a hundred years, with some still retaining an important connection with the railways in twenty-first century Britain. While modern trains may now be built abroad or under licence by overseas manufacturers on 'green field' sites like Newton Aycliffe in County Durham, some construction still takes place in traditional railway centres, even if the scope is much diminished. Today, Derby is the pre-eminent technical railway

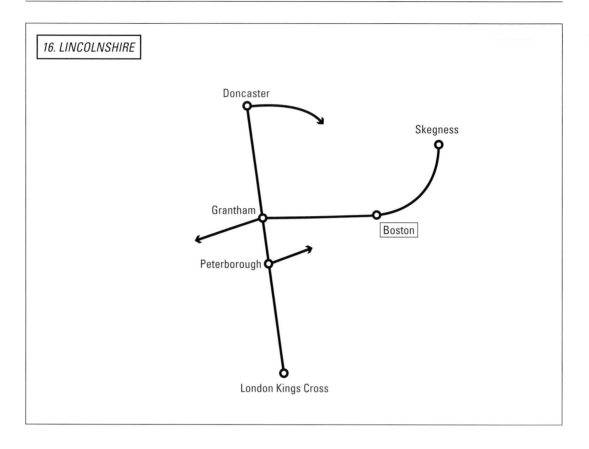

centre in Britain while Crewe, Doncaster, Swindon and Eastleigh all remain important rail industry centres.

When I grew up in the years before the Second World War the word Crewe was synonymous with every aspect of the railway industry. In 1837, the Grand Junction Railway arrived at what was then the small village of Crewe and for the next hundred years the workshops and assembly lines manufacturing steam engines and later diesels and electric locomotives, expanded. At the same time, miles of main line railway were developed and came to be controlled from the town. The locomotive workshops eventually spread across many square miles, while six major routes connected at Crewe, linking important centres like Liverpool, Manchester, Chester, Shrewsbury and Stoke on Trent to the west coast main line from London to Scotland. Nearly every train stopped at Crewe Station, giving connections to a vast number of destinations across the country. In 2013-14, over two and a half million people bought tickets to travel from the station, while at their peak Crewe works employed 20,000 people. Up until the mid-1960s, when steam power began to be replaced, over 7,000 locomotives had been built there.

Crewe's success was made possible because of the innovative approach adopted by Victorian managers and engineers who brooked no obstacles in their determination to ensure that their company would succeed. In 1853, Crewe began to make its own wrought iron while eight years later a Bessemer converter was built to enable the manufacture of steel. Men of vision like John Ramsbottom, a locomotive superintendent who designed the first steam safety valve in 1853 and later a device to allow a locomotive to collect water while on the move, and Sir William Stanier,

Bulk freight North Lincolnshire.

Upper Quadrant semaphore signal, Boston.

A cross country rural service at Grantham.

the LMS Chief Engineer who in the 1930s designed and built a range of highly efficient express steam locomotives, ensured that the LMS was always well to the fore when competing with its rivals after 1923, when the grouping of smaller lines led to the formation of the big four railway companies. During the Second World War, Crewe's workshops even built 150 battle tanks for the army.

Steam trains were always a dirty and temperamental form of transport and were rightly phased out when their function could be provided more easily, if not always more efficiently, by diesel or electric traction. But during their time they fulfilled a vital role and in so doing led the world in creating a transport system unrivalled since. The companies which developed the railways and established Crewe created one of the first 'all railway' towns in Britain and one of the most historic railway sites in the world.

St Botolph's Church, Boston

The Stump.

One of the largest parish churches in England with one of the tallest towers in the country, affectionately known as the Stump, a beacon for those travelling the Fens or sailing the treacherous waters of the Wash, and a starting point for many who emigrated to New England in the seventeenth century.

Look for the misericords in the choir, the 'mace rest' in front of the Mayor's pew, the doors leading into the nave at the south entrance and climb the 365 steps to the octagon lantern tower.

Boston lies amid flat, featureless Fenland country a few miles to the west of the Wash. Like so many Lincolnshire communities, the town's church stands like a sentinel over the surrounding countryside, in part beckoning people to worship within its precincts; in part giving them warning of any hostile marauders who might be approaching to disturb their peace and purpose which, given the wealthy trade once dispensed from Boston's port, was at times an ever present danger.

It is said that there has been a Christian community living and worshipping in the area since the seventh century, while the present church, dedicated to St Botolph, was begun in 1309. The church, built in the decorated style, was not finally completed until two centuries later when the tower was finished. The ruins of the previous Norman church lie under the south aisle.

St Botolph, an Anglo–Saxon missionary, is thought to have preached in Boston in the seventh century and founded a church there; the present day name of the town may be a corruption of the word 'Botolph'. Meanwhile, St Botolph's day is celebrated annually on 17 June. Boston was at the centre of an area of the Fens where sheep used to be grazed in their millions, producing wool which was then exported to Europe in a highly lucrative trade through the local port which, in its heyday, was one of the most prosperous in the country, only surpassed by London. Wealth generated by the wool trade may have led directly to the decision to build the current church. In some quarters it is contended that it is 'built on wool', a reference no doubt to this thriving medieval export trade, although a publication on sale in the church speculates that this could

The East Front.

equally refer to the fact that fleeces were sometimes used to bind building foundations during construction.

A visitor will be impressed with the church's light and airy interior and the width of its nave, both of which give an immediate feeling of wellbeing. Such is the nature of the ground on which the church stands, some of it silt washed up by the waters of the river Witham, that in the fifteenth century the chancel had to be extended to stabilise the building since when there has been no sign of further subsidence. However, it must be the tower, rising to 272 feet, which will immediately catch the eye of the visitor; why it was built to such a height and then topped off with an octagon lantern we shall probably never know. Standing at a point where Fenland starts to give way to the Lincolnshire Wolds, Boston's 'stump', as it universally known, rivals the equally prominent tower of Ely Cathedral, fifty miles to the south. The tower is thought to have been begun around 1450.

One of Boston's best known vicar's was John Cotton, a Congregationalist minister who presided over the affairs of the church in the early part of the seventeenth century. Following the Reformation and the disruption of the Civil War, the interior of St Botolph's sustained considerable damage with, as the church guide explains, 'pictures and statues and images and for their sake the windows and walls wherein they stood ... have been pulled down and broken in pieces and defaced ...' That was written in 1621 by Robert Sanderson following considerable damage by 'puritan rioters' that year. Like many churches, Boston suffered irreparable loss in the seventeenth and eighteenth centuries.

The window depicting the Revd John Cotton bidding farewell to pilgrims bound for America 1630.

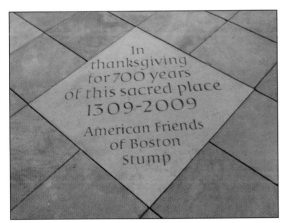

American Friends of the Stump commemoration stone.

It is however Boston's links to the New World which hold the greatest interest. A window in the north aisle shows various scenes connected with the early emigration of Bostonians to Massachusetts around 1630, including an image of Rev Cotton waving them farewell. In 1633, Cotton himself followed them to America where he became prominent in the Massachusetts church. Following refurbishment in 1857, the chapel west of the southern porch at Boston was renamed the Cotton chapel in his memory – a proposal to paint the roof with the Stars and Stripes was allegedly dismissed by the vicar at the time as 'popish'! Nearby, there is a memorial under the tower to several Lincolnshire men who rose to high positions in the government of Boston 'across the pond'. In emphasis of the continuing connection between the two Bostons, in recent years much of the restoration work undertaken in St Botolph's has been generously supported by help from America.

The resting place for the Mayor of Boston's mace.

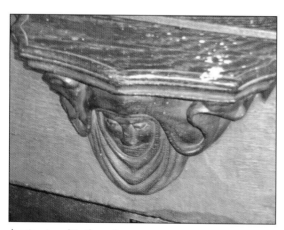

A misericord in the quire.

In front of the first pews at the head of the nave on the left hand side is the Mayor's pew. Directly in front and attached to the pew is a rest where his mace is placed when he attends a service; it is brightly coloured although the detail might be thought rather lurid; it dates from 1727. Opposite is the pulpit, beautifully worked and given to the church in 1612 by the town Corporation when John Cotton was appointed as vicar.

Beyond the nave altar, introduced in 1984, is the quire and chancel. The quire stalls probably date from 1390 and their canopies, resembling those in Lincoln Cathedral, were added in 1853 during a later period of church restoration. The sixty-two misericords are decorated with images of men and animals, a wonderful collection of medieval carvings. Boston's collection is amongst the finest in the country. Further east is the high altar with the reredos depicting Christ on the Cross surrounded by figures of

The quire and east window.

saints with the Last Supper depicted below. It was dedicated in 1891 to Walter Scrivener, who had drowned twelve years earlier, and was finished in 1914.

Most of the church's stained glass has been installed within the last two hundred years, some of it designed by C E Kempe, whose work is found in many churches restored in the late nineteenth century. The east window, although hidden by the reredos, and the windows in the north aisle are of particular interest. A feature of the church, mentioned in the parish's own leaflet 'Why Boston Stump?' is the coincidence of so many statistics corresponding to certain familiar numbers in constant use in our everyday lives: 365 steps to the top of the tower; 24 steps to the library above the south porch; 12 pillars supporting the roof; 7 doors, 52 windows and 60 steps to the roof above the chancel. There is no record to show that these 'calendar numbers' may have been intentional and of course subsequent restoration may have rendered them no longer correct. However they are an interesting facet of the church.

Boston may be a long way from Britain's main rail and road arteries but it has much to interest the traveller and is well worth the journey to reach it. Its tower, and the opportunity to explore the connection between Boston in Lincolnshire and one of America's oldest and finest cities, is reason enough to go there. John Betjeman in the Collins *Guide to English Parish Churches* comments, 'one of the largest, and in some respects the grandest, of all parish churches in England …with the loftiest tower in England.'

North Norfolk Railway

Class 5 steam locomotive on the North Norfolk Railway.

Holt, North Norfolk Railway.

Coupling up.

Chapter 17

Suffolk

▪ The future for railways across the world ▪ **All Saints Church, Long Melford** ▪

Getting There

A journey of one hour will take the traveller from Liverpool Street on the Great Eastern mainline to Mark's Tey near Colchester. From there it takes twenty minutes to Sudbury on the branch line and a short bus or taxi ride to Long Melford, less than five miles distant.

Railway Notes

This book has already touched upon aspects of how Britain's railways have been developed and improved over the twenty years since privatisation in 1997 and has argued that, so long as financial provision can be found, further modernisation will be of considerable benefit to the nation. This should include not only further high speed rail projects but also more efficient use of the existing network. Evidently, much will depend upon establishing high quality, experienced management teams to lead change, one example being the team charged with handling the future high speed rail programme, its delivery on time, within financial forecasts and with minimum effect on the environment. One of the criticisms levelled at the railway industry since 1997 has been that too many professional railwaymen have been excluded from the decision making. With so much happening in a highly specialised industry, now must surely be the time to ensure their knowledge and talents are not wasted. Meanwhile, unambiguous political leadership and support will be as important if national plans are to be fulfilled.

Across the world, careful deliberation as to how rail transportation can be developed is taking place. The Japanese, who built the first high speed 'bullet trains' or *Sinkansen* (new trunk lines) are researching further technologies to provide even faster train services; their first lines created in 1964 were capable of speeds of between 150 and 200 miles per hour running on dedicated tracks and now cover 1,625 route miles. The Chinese are equally experimenting with similar trains capable of 270 mph or more, while America, a nation not known for its attachment to its railroads since the Second World War – instead preferring the independence and greater convenience conferred by the motor car and the aeroplane – is beginning to plan some conventional high speed lines, notably one running between Los Angeles and San Francisco. Magnetic levitation, a system whereby vehicles travel on super conducting rails above a bed of air and capable of delivering even higher speeds, is amongst innovative ideas being considered. However, such systems are expensive to build and maintain.

The term 'hyper speed' is now being heard in the research world and Hyperloop, a revolutionary American concept for overland travel has claimed the possibility of a train 'which can never crash, is immune to weather, twice as fast as an aeroplane, four times as fast as a high speed conventional train and which can be run completely on solar power'. A visionary view of things to come or

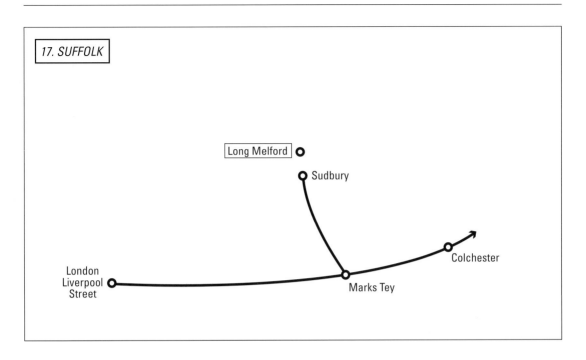

17. SUFFOLK

Long Melford

Sudbury

Colchester

London
Liverpool
Street

Marks Tey

A Japanese Sinkansen train in the NRM, York

simply a researcher's hyperbole? What is however relevant is that some of the foremost engineers and visionaries in the world of transport engineering are thinking about such revolutionary concepts.

Britain has neither the space not the requirement for such futuristic schemes but is now planning to build further high speed routes following that completed in 1994 between the Channel Tunnel and London. Many remain to be convinced of the wisdom and the necessity of such schemes, citing the environmental and financial consequences of their construction. However some factors relevant to the debate need to be considered before judgements are reached. In Europe high speed trains running on dedicated tracks have improved passenger services and general mobility while experience suggests that new high speed routes will in future be implemented if the travelling public see them to be both convenient and desirable, something which may now be starting to happen in America. In parallel, attention is turning to providing dedicated freight routes where the transport of bulk loads and domestic imports between port and distribution centre can be effected more economically, more efficiently and more profitably than in individual lorry loads and, if carefully planned, with less impact on the environment. Depending upon oil prices, rail transport can in many instances be a more cost effective provider than road, especially if electrical locomotion is used.

The debate about Britain's future transport options will rage for years to come and there is unlikely ever to be a right solution. Maybe the best permutation will be strategic rail and local road but ultimately the outcome must depend upon what those living on this small and increasingly crowded island cherish most: a highly efficient transport system which allows them to move where and when they wish but which will in the process demand increased infrastructure, or the preservation of the environment to the exclusion of other developments. Our way of life is already under threat from numerous directions and the debate about how we live will never be silenced, because change is inexorable. This is as true of transportation as any other sphere and it will need wisdom and courage by existing and later generations to strike a balance between opposing visions of the future. However, so much is already altering rapidly in the field of electronics, be it in personal communications, military systems and space exploration, to name but three industries that new transport technology is unlikely to lag far behind.

Since the Beeching report of fifty years ago, successive British governments have never seriously attempted to devise a blueprint for railway development and as a result what plans there have been, have tended to emerge piecemeal and often as a reaction to a particular circumstance. Following the construction of the Channel Tunnel and the building of High Speed One, the current discussion and planning of both High Speed Two to connect northwards from London and an abundance of smaller proposed schemes, a more co-ordinated approach to identifying the nation's future transport requirements has started to emerge. Let us hope that political leaders of the future will use wisdom and courage to find practical answers to what will often appear to be intractable problems of development, as their Victorian predecessors did two centuries before them.

All Saints Church, Long Melford

An elegant and pleasing church, set on rising ground at the north end of Long Melford village in one of Suffolk's most rural districts and close to where Constable painted many of his works.

Look for the glass in the north aisle, the Clopton family chapel and tombs, the memorial to the Hyde Parker family and the Lady Chapel.

L ong Melford, on the northern edge of 'Constable country', was important in the Middle Ages for its role as a wool town, a centre of the cloth trade similar to places like Cirencester and Boston.

The Domesday Book confirmed that Long Melford had a church in 1086 but little is known about the details of what the Saxons and later the Normans may have built, although the nave arcades may give some clues. Three great East Anglian wool families – the Cloptons, the Cordells and the Martyns – were largely responsible for today's church at Long Melford which was completed in 1484, with the Clopton family carrying out much of the early work. Today, the church presents a most attractive sight as you approach across the village green and past some Tudor alms houses, originally built as a sixteenth century hospital; the church lies stretched out, longer than some cathedrals, with a tower at the west end and a Lady Chapel to the east, one of the few parish churches to be built with one; it was completed in 1496. The original tower was

The Church viewed from the south.

The entrance.

Looking east.

destroyed by lightning in 1710, rebuilt fifteen years later, but was again restructured in 1903 as part of the village's commemoration of the Diamond Jubilee of Queen Victoria of 1887, a parish project which would have required considerable time and resources to complete. The church is the only one described in this book built of flint stone.

Inside, the church is light and airy with much clear glass. What stained glass that exists is mostly on the north side, much of the original glass having been destroyed at the time of the Reformation or the Civil War. What was left was later consolidated in windows at the east and west ends before being moved in the middle of the twentieth century into the north aisle. Near the north door is a tiny section of glass depicting three hares, each with two ears but only three between them. The Hare window is a small roundel immediately above the door and is believed to signify the Holy Trinity. Similar symbols are said to have been found in China around 600 and again there are apparently some examples of wooden bosses with similar symbols in some churches in Devon. To discover how the three hares can be united in a window with only three ears you will need to visit Long Melford.

Close by to the left of the door is a window showing Elizabeth Talbot, the Duchess of Norfolk. One account has it that the image was used by John Tenniel for the duchess in *Alice in Wonderland*. Further to the east on the north side of the church is the Singing Tower, a brick turret rather

The image of Elizabeth Talbot, said to be the model for the Duchess in *Alice in Wonderland*.

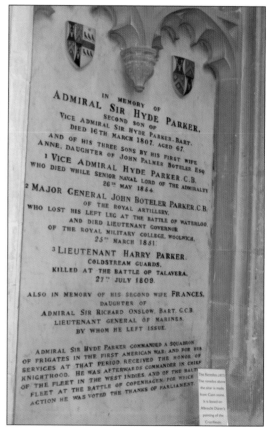

The Hyde Parker family memorial.

The font.

incongruously positioned on the outside of the building but once accessible from inside. How it came by its name is unclear.

The Clopton family had their own chapel and chantry on the north side of the chancel and there are several tombs commemorating the family who did so much for the church; according to the guidebook at one time they held their own services in their chapel in parallel with those being held in the church and conducted by their own appointed priest, who would look through a squint in order to co-ordinate with the priest at the high altar. Apparently the Clopton family priest lived in the church, sleeping in what is now the priest's vestry. Both the Martyn and Cordell families, equally important benefactors, are commemorated in the church.

A more recent family associated with the church are the Hyde Parkers who have lived at Long Melford Hall since 1786. A memorial to the left of the chancel records Admiral Hyde Parker who commanded several naval task forces or squadrons at the time of the Napoleonic Wars and who is purported to have sent a signal to Admiral Nelson during the battle of Copenhagen in 1801 to which the latter is famously said 'to have turned a blind eye'. The admiral died in 1807 but his three sons went on to achieve military distinction in other fields.

As already mentioned, the Lady Chapel, a feature more often associated with cathedrals or abbeys than parish churches, is at the east end but only accessible from outside through a door on the south side. Roofed with red tiles the chapel is large and sparsely decorated, possibly the only one in Britain to be found as part of a parish church which was itself not originally an abbey. On a wall at the east end is a faded wall inscription setting out a set of multiplication tables, evidence of the chapel having been used as the village school for over a hundred years from 1670 until about 1800. The chapel is highly praised by John Betjeman as 'the marvellous Lady Chapel surrounded by an ambulatory with a wonderful tie-beam roof all the way round' His praise for the church overall is equally fulsome and he extols many of the internal features of the building and its adornments in the Collins *Guide to Parish Churches*.

All Saints in Long Melford is one of the most handsome buildings I visited. Lovely to behold from the outside and interesting inside for what it tells us about those aristocratic families in the shires who influenced rural life and to a large extent prescribed the practices of their church during much of the latter half of the second millennium. Visited on a wet summer afternoon with showers and alternating glimpses of bright sunshine, the church and its surrounds presented a picture, quintessentially English in character and wonderfully reassuring to those to whom Christian worship remains so important.

Railway Notes

Having arrived on a fast electric train at Mark's Tey, the traveller wishing to reach Sudbury must transfer into a diesel railcar to travel to Sudbury, a distance of ten miles. This is a distinct contrast to the journey from London and shows how some of our more rural and only marginally profitable branch lines can still be kept in use in an age of austerity. The line is run as 'a basic railway' with only one train ever on the route – known in railway jargon as 'one engine in steam' – thereby minimising any the risk of collision, with unmanned stations and no signalling. This allows a train to shuttle back and forth costing little more than the fuel to propel it and the expense of the driver and conductor manning the service. Such an unglamorous railway is small price to pay for the convenience of a continuing link to a community which might otherwise have little other public transport provision. (See also Chapter 12).

The Sudbury branch, a shuttle railcar.

The Great Eastern mainline at Marks Tey.

Chapter 18

Essex

Getting There

A train from Liverpool Street to Waltham Cross (the nearest station to Waltham Abbey) takes under thirty minutes. The abbey is then a five minute drive although equally feasible on foot. An alternative route from Central London is to take a Victoria Line train to Tottenham Hale and to connect into the Liverpool Street train from there.

Railway Notes

The final chapter of the companion volume to this book, *England's Cathedrals by Train*, reviewed some of the plans either already made or in prospect for improving rail transport services in London and the South East of England. Since then, these plans have advanced with the local authority for the nation's capital, the Mayor of London, taking wider responsibility for transport. As a result many of the conurbation's heavy rail, surface routes are now managed by the Mayor's office – branded as London Overground – clearly defining them as a sister organisation to London Underground, the already well established company overseeing the operation of underground or tube trains, also managed by the Mayor's office. These moves, along with County Hall's control of London's buses, have resulted in better co-ordinated and more modern transport services across the capital, something long overdue.

Crossrail is the name given to the Government's current project to build a railway across London from west to east to allow uninterrupted travel, eliminating the necessity to change trains or transfer from one mode of travel to another. Once completed, the new route will link Reading, thirty-six miles to the west of the capital, and Heathrow Airport, with destinations in Essex and North Kent. Commuters and airline passengers will be amongst the principal beneficiaries.

The section of Crossrail passing under the centre of London in tunnels is twenty-six miles in length. A train coming from the Reading direction will enter the western portal of the underground section at Royal Oak prior to reaching Paddington station, and will emerge in the east at either Pudding Mill Lane to connect with the existing line to Shenfield and Stratford, or, in the former Victoria Dock area to link into rail routes to North Kent at Woolwich. It has taken three years to bore the tunnels using eight massive Tunnel Boring Machines or TBMs, each completing sections of the route which will now be fitted out with the necessary high speed infrastructure.

Creating tunnels under a city as complex as London with all its existing subterranean facilities, has been difficult, to say the least. Existing water mains, sewers, cabling services and other underground rail tunnels had all to be avoided while the foundations of the many massive buildings found in a city like London, have had to be protected. The TBMs each weighed about 1,000 tonnes and had to be manoeuvred with considerable skill to avoid colliding with the services

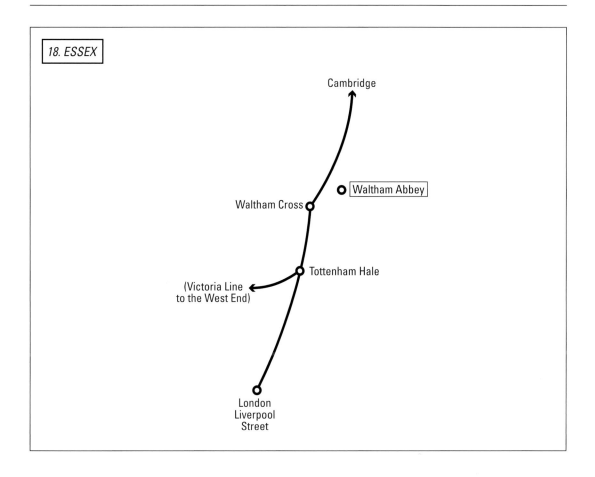

18. ESSEX

Cambridge

Waltham Abbey

Waltham Cross

Tottenham Hale

(Victoria Line
to the West End)

London
Liverpool
Street

described above. Each TBM was 148 feet long and was an equivalent size to fourteen London buses. The tunnels are forty-two metres below the surface. Over 200,000 concrete segments, each weighing over three tonnes, have been used to line the tunnels. Finally 3.4 million tonnes of spoil have so far been excavated of which 3 million have been taken by barge to Wallasea island in Essex, creating a wetland nature reserve twice the size of the City of London.

What happens now? The overall project is about two thirds complete and the fitting out of the tunnels will now take place: 'finishing' each bore, laying track, connecting overhead power cables, installing the signalling and safety systems and completing the stations which will serve the capital's central area, will all need to be co-ordinated in an overall plan. Stations at Bond Street and Tottenham Court Road, hitherto known only as stops on the Victoria or Northern Underground lines, will soon become main line stations, for example, allowing travel direct from Heathrow airport to Oxford Street.

Looking further ahead there are already embryonic plans to enhance London's transport infrastructure by building a second Crossrail link from south west to north east beneath the city. Meanwhile the ultimate decision as to which of the existing London airports should be expanded to meet an ever increasing demand for flights, or whether an entirely new airport should be constructed, will inevitably have an impact on future rail plans. A new or expanded airport will only be truly valid if it is part of a single, fully integrated transport system planned and built to serve the needs of London and the nation for decades to come.

Waltham Abbey

A once great church reduced in status and size in the sixteenth century.

Look for the painted roof panels and the glass at the east end including the east window by Edward Burne Jones.

Once an important church, the abbey at Waltham, like so many other once great medieval institutions, is but a shadow of what it was following considerable reduction in size at the time of the Dissolution. It is purported to have been the last of the monasteries to have been dissolved by Henry VIII's commissioners, the local people having delayed the process by claiming that the church represented their place of worship and that they should be allowed to retain it.

Today, the abbey church is situated in a quiet corner on the edge of London's outer suburbs, just across a boundary in Essex. There had been a church in Waltham since the seventh century, although little is known about it except that around 1050 Harold Godwinson, later King Harold,

The view of the Abbey from the east.

East end and high altar.

The Abbey.

replaced it with a new structure. It was apparently in this church that he sought God's blessing before the Battle of Hastings in 1066 and where his body was brought after his defeat at the hands of William I. His grave is believed to be to the east of the church.

After the establishment of a monastic community by Harold, little happened until 1177, when Henry II ordered an increase in the size of the monastery and the recruitment of twenty-six Augustinian monks. This royal gesture was allegedly a reaction to the murder seven years previously of Archbishop Thomas Becket in Canterbury cathedral, for which Henry later felt remorse and wished to do penance.

After 1540, the only part of the building to be left standing was the nave. The tower was erected in 1556 during the reign of Mary, the elder daughter of Henry VIII, primarily to prevent the rest of the building collapsing. It was the only church tower built during Mary's reign and then only to ensure the stability of the church. The original outline of the monastery can still be detected in the grounds surrounding the present church but otherwise there is little to indicate the size and splendour of the original buildings.

There are similarities in the way that Waltham Abbey and a priory church like that at Bridlington were truncated after the Dissolution to allow only the retention of the nave for local worship. The nave roof and the east end of today's church at Waltham are Victorian; the roof painted by Edward Poynter in 1860 includes a number of panels showing the twelve signs of the Zodiac. They signify the passage of time and have their origin in pagan lore, in time being appropriated by the church

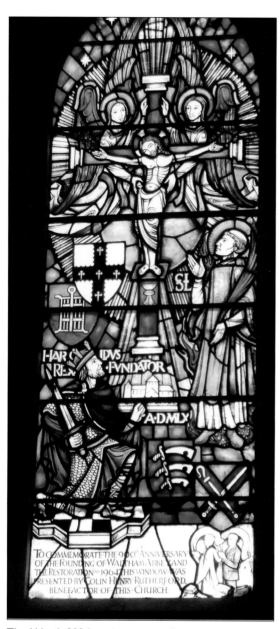

The Abbey's 900th anniversary window.

which then gave them a Christian meaning. Aquarius, 'the water carrier' signifies baptism while Gemini 'twins' depicts the duality of Christ both human and divine. John Betjeman in the Collins *Guide* describes the nave as splendid, comparing it to that of Durham Cathedral.

The east window was restored during a major programme of work in 1859. A rose window denoting Creation and, beneath it, the three lancet Jesse window, were designed by Edward Burne-Jones; the two side lancets show the prophets and the Kings of Judah while the central lancet follows Christ's ancestry from Jesse through King David to Christ. A small brightly coloured window at the east end of the north aisle commemorates the 900th anniversary of the building of the nave and the restoration work carried out in 1964.

The Lady Chapel is on the south side at the east end of the Church and below is the undercroft, originally a funeral guild chapel dating from the fourteenth century. On the east wall of the Lady Chapel is a fifteenth century 'Doom' painting depicting the Day of Judgement, an understandably gloomy interpretation of how people might have foreseen that event in the Middle Ages.

Had Henry VIII not embarked upon a policy calculated to reduce the status and influence of the Roman Catholic Church in the sixteenth century, thereby depriving its monasteries of their wealth and purpose, Waltham Abbey might well today still be the imposing and important church it once was. Its presence in a small Home Counties town – barely distinguishable from those other places around it – and now left with a role only that of a parish church, should cause us to think back to the early years of the sixteenth century and the repercussions of a royal prince contracting 'sweating sickness' thereby destining him for an early grave. That is not to argue that the fate of the Church and its monastic settlements would not have been as eventually occurred had Prince Arthur survived in April 1502, but the manner of the Dissolution and the final outcome for the religious establishment in England could have been vastly different.

Epilogue

That the sixteenth century was a period of unprecedented change in English history will already be known by those who read this book. While the teaching of history by our schools may no longer cover the events and consequences of Henry VIII's reign in the detail it once did, the recent emergence of books and films chronicling the lives of the Tudors will have added greatly to the general knowledge of that era. It was a period of great unrest, unpredictable events and human tragedy; for most people it was a time of dark bewilderment when it probably paid not to think too deeply about the events going on around you and certainly a time to avoid becoming caught up in them. Henry VIII was a callous, despotic ruler, terrified lest the intrigues and the hatred which his reign gave rise to should overwhelm him, distrustful of all but a few advisers and seemingly confident in his own mind that he was ordained to be God's chosen representative in England, a position he created for himself when he finally severed formal links with the Roman Catholic Church.

The churches reviewed here were all affected to some degree by Henry's policy of Dissolution and Reformation in the period after 1530, as they were further disturbed over a hundred years later when England was ruled for nine years by the Puritan dictator, Oliver Cromwell. That the great churches selected in this book and their worshipping communities survived two such far reaching upheavals in such a short period of time, says much for their durability and the care bestowed upon them – both then and since – by devoted congregations. Originally built by men of resolve and maintained over the intervening centuries by others of equal purpose, is there any reason to doubt that they will not still be standing in five hundred or even a thousand years' time?

But can the same be said of the country's railways? Will they survive another two hundred years or more or will they be swept away by a revolutionary system of transport not yet envisaged by mankind? Fifty years ago, the future for rail indeed looked bleak as Dr Beeching and others set about pruning the network in favour of the motor car and the aeroplane; but not today when, despite the birth pangs of 'privatisation' and later instances of management shortcomings, the future looks far more assured. A land based system of fast and efficient surface travel over medium to long distances, superintended in a controlled and effective manner to meet the requirements of all those living in these increasingly crowded islands, will always be needed and as of today there is little to say that railways may not be that system.

As you go around the country to discover the wonderful buildings described in these pages and you contemplate their history and what they represent – and you do so travelling at a speed and in comfort unimaginable to our forbears - think about the heritage that the early Christians, the Normans, the Victorians and others in between originally created and have now entrusted to us to maintain and to hand on to succeeding generations.

Bibliography

The official guidebooks, companion guides and associated literature published for sale by the churches visited.

BARRINGTON TATFORD, *The Story of British Railways.* Sampson Low, Marston & Co, London, 1945.

BETJEMAN, John *Guide to English Parish Churches* , Collins, London 1958.

JENKINS, Simon. *England's Thousand Best Churches.* Allen Lane, The Penguin Press 1999.

NAYLOR, Murray. *England's Cathedrals by Train.* Pen & Sword Books, Barnsley 2013.

ROLT, LTC *Red for Danger.* Pan Books, London, 1967.

ROWLAND, John, *George Stephenson, Creator of Britain's Railways.* Odhams Press, London 1954.

SIMMONS, Jack & BIDDLE, Gordon (eds) *The Oxford Companion to British Railway History* Oxford University Press 1997.

Index

Locators for pictures indicated in "**bold**"

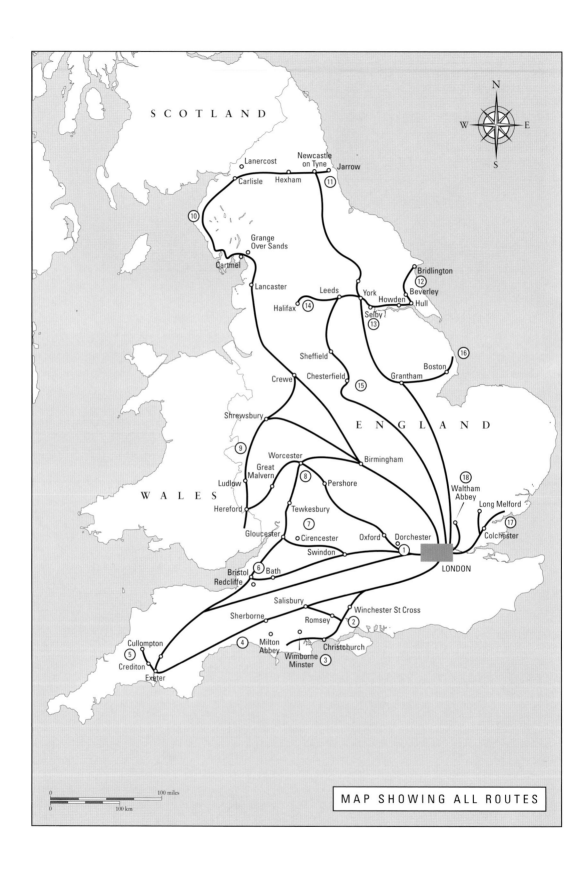

MAP SHOWING ALL ROUTES

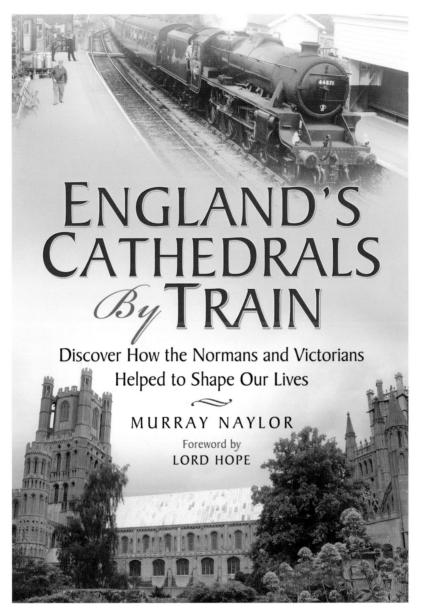

England's Cathedrals by Train – Murray Naylor

ISBN 9781783030286

RRP £25.00

Available from all good bookshops or from Pen & Sword Books Ltd.
Call 01226 734222 or visit www.pen–and–sword.co.uk